THE SHANNON'S BRIGADE IN INDIA

THE SHANNON'S BRIGADE IN INDIA

EDMUND HOPE VERNEY

GYAN

Published by

Gyan Publishing House
5, Ansari Road
Daryaganj, New Delhi-110002
Phone: 011-47034999, 9811692060
E-mail: books@gyanbooks.com

Distribution Network
gyanbooks.com
India, USA, Canada, UK, Australia

ISBN: 978-93-7133-549-2 (PB)

First Published, 1862

2nd Impression 2025

Printed at: Gyan Press, Delhi.

THE SHANNON'S BRIGADE IN INDIA
Author: EDMUND HOPE VERNEY

THE SHANNON'S BRIGADE IN INDIA

THE

SHANNON'S BRIGADE IN INDIA

BEING SOME ACCOUNT OF
SIR WILLIAM PEEL'S NAVAL BRIGADE IN
THE INDIAN CAMPAIGN OF

1857–1858

BY

EDMUND HOPE VERNEY

LIEUT. R.N.

LONDON
SAUNDERS, OTLEY, AND CO.
66 BROOK STREET, HANOVER SQUARE
1862

To the Memory of

SIR WILLIAM PEEL

AND TO THE

OFFICERS AND BLUE-JACKETS OF HIS NAVAL BRIGADE

Are Dedicated

THESE RECOLLECTIONS OF OUR INDIAN CAMPAIGN

PREFACE.

In offering this book to the public, I do not profess to give a history of the Indian Mutiny, or even of a small portion of it. I can only write a description of the scenes witnessed by one individual of a large army, and give the reports of operations which he did *not* witness as they often reached him, some incorrectly, others perhaps utterly without foundation.

I cannot but feel that no small responsibility attaches to one who attempts to print an account, however crude, of the deeds of such a man as Sir William Peel, or of his blue jackets; but as, after a lapse of three years, none has yet appeared, I trust that my simple narrative may not be considered inappropriate as a slight memento of a portion of the last services of our lamented commander.

In preparing these pages for publication, I have adhered to the form of a journal, although, not considered the most readable style for a book, because they are compiled from letters and journals written at the time.

During our year's campaign in India, one feeling pervaded the minds of the officers of the Naval Brigade, which only strengthened as time went on, and an expression of which cannot possibly be omitted here. This was the obligation we all felt we were under to the whole army, from the Commander-in-Chief down to the naughty drummer-boy who (afraid of getting licked by his comrades) sounded the "advance" at Kallee-Nuddee without orders, for their unremitting consideration and civility to every officer or blue jacket of ours. Had a sentry orders only to admit a favoured few to the roof of the Dilkushah, he would stretch a point in favour of the crown and anchor button; were baggage-camels to be issued, the Naval Brigade were first served; did we want medical assistance, a surgeon from the Staff was sent to us; we had only to ask for a thing to get it; and was one of our men a little "disguised" and in trouble — as even sailors will be sometimes — he was quietly handed over to his own officers to be settled with; and although thus openly favoured, in no instance did any feeling of jealously appear, but all seemed animated with a desire to show to blue jackets on land the civility and hospitality which I trust we always endeavour to show to red coats afloat.

I must not neglect this opportunity of tendering my sincere thanks to the Shannon's late chaplain, for his kindness in allowing me the use of his journal, and to Mrs. Verschoyle, the lady to whose kindness and skill I am indebted for the photograph of Sir William Peel, which does duty as frontispiece.

In sending these pages to the press, I cannot foresee whether they will be cast upon the already swollen heap of unread books, or be deemed worthy of a happier fate; but once launched into print, copies *may* be stranded on the shores where the scenes are laid, and I hope these lines may meet the eyes of those whose cordial hospitality and good-fellowship, to my brother officers and myself, have left recollections which I assure them will not easily be effaced. But deeper still, in my own mind, lies the remembrance of the affectionate kindness of those intimate friends, in whose superior and elevating society were spent many successive Sundays or Friday evenings, and unmindful of whom I can never, in word or thought, refer to my year in India.

CLAYDON HOUSE: *Nov.* 16, 1861.

CONTENTS.

LIST OF ILLUSTRATIONS.

THE SHANNON'S BRIGADE IN INDIA.

CHAPTER I.

A SHORT SKETCH OF THE PROCEEDINGS OF H. M. S. SHANNON, FROM THE DATE OF HER BEING COMMISSIONED TO HER ARRIVAL AT CALCUTTA.

HER Majesty's screw steam frigate Shannon, of 51 guns, 600 horse-power, and 2667 tons, was commissioned by Captain William Peel at Portsmouth on the 13th of September, 1856. At this time she was the finest frigate afloat, being the first of a new and very powerful class, calculated to obtain great speed under sail or steam, and to carry very heavy metal. Her armament consisted of twenty 56 cwt. 32-prs. on the upper deck, one 95 cwt. 68-pr. on the forecastle, and thirty 65 cwt. 8-in. guns on the main deck, and she could steam twelve knots.

After she was fitted out she went round to Plymouth Sound, and, as if destined for adventure from the very commencement of her career, was nearly lost there on the 3rd of January of the ensuing year. At about 6 A.M. a strong westerly gale sprung up, and it became necessary to veer cable, as the ship was lying at single anchor. In doing this the cable parted, and the other anchor was at once let go: quickly, however, though this was done, from the great force of the wind the ship had already gathered sternway, and, to everybody's consternation, the second cable also snapped. There was but one other cable bent, the starboard sheet, and that anchor could not be let go at once. All hands were turned up to clear it away, and Captain Peel rushed on deck in his shirt and trowsers. In the meantime the ship was drifting rapidly to the eastward, with her broadside to the wind. Owing to the great personal exertions of the first lieutenant, Mr. Vaughan, the sheet anchor was presently cleared away and let go, and providentially it brought the ship up, or she must have left her bones on the rocks below Bovisand.

The Shannon was ordered to Lisbon; but on the 10th of January, off Ushant, in a strong westerly breeze, the step of the mainmast was discovered to be sprung, and the ship returned to Plymouth, where she remained for a long time in dock. When again ready for sea, she went for a cruise off Cape Clear, and returned to Spithead. She was now ordered to prepare for service in China, and left England on the 17th of March, 1857.

The Shannon's outward voyage was attended by no remarkable incident. Three times between England and the Cape a man fell overboard, and on each occasion her boats, fitted with Clifford's lowering apparatus, were manned and lowered with great celerity, and on two occasions the men were saved. The third case was that of Mr. J. Coaker, master's assistant, a most promising young Greenwich scholar, who fell off the fore-yard, but his head striking the fore-chains, he was killed before reaching the water. His body was picked up and brought on board, and in the evening was committed to the deep, sewn up in a hammock, with two 32-pr. shot at his feet, and covered by the union jack; the body was brought up on a grating with his cap and dirk placed over the breast. All the officers attended, the ship's company on the gangway, the marines on the quarter-deck, and the band playing the "Dead March in Saul." The Rev. E. L. Bowman read the funeral service; and at the words "we therefore commit his body to the deep," the remains of poor young Coaker glanced over the side and plunged into the sea.

The Shannon anchored in Simon's Bay on the 7th of May, and sailed again on the 11th. About the 20th of the month, in a strong north-westerly gale, the speed of the ship under canvas was very remarkable; under double-reefed topsails, courses, and reefed fore-topmast studding-sail, the ship sometimes averaged fourteen and fifteen knots an hour; and, during one squall, when the log was hove by the officer of the watch, she was going 15·8.

On the 11th of June, the Shannon anchored off Singapore. On her arrival here the first intimation was received of the outbreak in India; and the Simoom, arriving with troops for China, was ordered to return with them to Calcutta; so she steamed out, the military band on board playing "You may go to Hong Kong for me." On the 23rd Lord Elgin embarked with his suite, and the Shannon sailed for Hong Kong, where she arrived on the 2nd of July.

On the 16th, hearing that affairs in India were assuming a very troublous aspect, the Earl of Elgin and suite re-embarked; and, taking on board a detachment of Royal Marines, and of the 90th Regiment, sailed for Calcutta, touching at Singapore *en route.*

On the 6th of August the Shannon arrived off the mouths of the Ganges. The water here is very shallow, and the low mud shore cannot be perceived from any distance, so the most careful navigation is requisite. Soundings were obtained, the ship put under easy sail, a gun fired, and a jack hoisted for a pilot. The Calcutta pilot service is a distinct service in itself, under martial law like the royal navy, and turns out many a good seaman and steady officer, and the pilots receive half-pay and retiring pensions after a certain term of service. At length a smart little brig came under the

Shannon's stern, lowered a boat, aad sent a pilot on board: and the frigate, furling sails, steamed through the dull and muddy waters to the mouth of the Hooghly. The scenery of that part of the Delta formed by the mouths of the Ganges called the Sunderbunds, is anything but inviting: from the mast-head of a large ship, as far as the eye can reach, no rise of land is visible in any direction; at high water the sea is almost on a level with the tops of the innumerable mud islands, and which are uninhabited save by crocodiles and a few wild beasts; they are covered with a thick and almost impenetrable jungle, and there are seen the gigantic leaves and luxuriant vegetation of a tropical climate. This description of scenery continues to within a few miles of Calcutta itself, varied only by occasional mud flats, from which arise pestilential odours in the hot season. On nearing Calcutta, the east bank of the river, called Garden Reach, is covered with villas and pleasure-grounds; here are the head-quarters of the Peninsular and Oriental Company, while nearly opposite are the grey buildings of Bishop's College; on passing these, and the frowning batteries and green slopes of Fort William, the Shannon was repeatedly cheered,—for at this time every English arm was cordially welcomed; and the opportune arrival of two men-of-war, the Shannon and Pearl, whose heavy guns could sweep the Maidân, gave confidence to the anxious hearts of India's rulers, and seemed to take a load off every European mind; and at 5 P.M., as the frigate's anchor dropped from her bows, and the governor-general's salute of nineteen guns thundered through the sultry air, echoing and re-echoing on the walls of Government House, it may have suggested a hint of England's might to the Despot of Oude, now a captive in Fort William.

At Calcutta, Lord Elgin disembarked; he afterwards chartered the steamer Ava, and returned in her to China. In the meantime, Captain Peel offered to the governor-general the services of the blue jackets of the Shannon, with their ships' guns, to form a Naval Brigade, which were accepted, and preparations for service on shore immediately begun; the dress of the men was in no respect altered, but their straw hats were covered with white cotton, and provided with curtains to protect the back of the neck. On the 12th of August, Dr. Wilson, Lord Bishop of Calcutta, visited the ship; after going all over her, the ship's company assembled on the quarter-deck, and he addressed them energetically, saying, that if he were not eighty-four years of age, he would go up to fight the Sepoys himself. On the 13th, a large flat came alongside the Shannon, and was laden with ten 8-inch guns and two brass field-pieces, with a proportion of ammunition, and a supply of clothing and medical comforts for the men. The great rivers of India are its main arteries of commerce, which is carried on by means of steamers, or flats towed by them; these flats have great beam, but do not draw more than two foot, or two foot six; they are thatched over to keep out the burning sun, and are available for the navigation of the rivers at all seasons of the year. On the 14th, the river-steamer Chunar came alongside the frigate, and Captain Peel embarked, with the following officers: Lieuts. Young, Wilson, Hay, and Salmon; Captain Gray and Lieut. Stirling, R.M.; Lieut. Lind, of Hageby, of the Swedish navy; the Rev. E. L. Bowman; Dr. Flanagan; Mr. Comerford, assistant-paymaster; Messrs. M. Daniel, Garvey, E. Daniel, Lord Walter Kerr, Lord Arthur Clinton, and Mr. Church, midshipmen; Messrs. Brown, Bone, and Henri, engineers; Mr. Thompson, gunner; Mr. Bryce, carpenter; Mr. Stanton, assistant-clerk; and Messrs. Watson and Lascelles, naval cadets. Four hundred and fifty men, with their arms and ammunition, embarked in the flat, which was taken in tow by the Chunar: Captain Peel also took up a launch and cutter belonging to the Shannon. The ship was left under the command of Mr. Vaughan, the first lieutenant; and as the Chunar steamed away, three hearty cheers were exchanged.

From this time the officers left on board the Shannon were daily employed volunteering men from English merchant ships in the river; and in this manner one hundred men were raised, and immediately put through a course of drill.

On the 12th of September, Captain Sotheby, R.N., started for the interior, with one hundred and fifty-five of the ship's company of H.M.S. Pearl,—an account of whose proceedings has been published by her chaplain, the Rev. E. A. Williams.

On the morning of the 18th, the river steamer Benares, with a flat in tow, came alongside the Shannon, and Lieut. Vaughan embarked on board of her, with the following officers: Lieut. Wratislaw; Mr. Verney, mate; Mr. Way, midshipman; and Mr. Richards, naval cadet; one hundred and twenty men embarked in the flat, with their rifles and ammunition. As this reinforcement steamed away up the Hooghly, they gave the old ship three cheers, which were stoutly returned by the little party left on board. The frigate was left under the command of Mr. Waters, master, with about one hundred and forty men, moored close to the shore, and a brass gun was mounted in the main-top to sweep the Maidân in case of any disturbance in Calcutta.

The further proceedings of this detachment, afterwards called the first company, and a general sketch of the movements of the Shannon's Naval Brigade, are detailed in the pages of the following journal.

CHAP. II.

JOURNEY TO ALLAHABAD IN THE RIVER STEAMER BENARES.

♀ *September* 18*th.*—This morning the steamer Benares with a flat in tow came alongside the Shannon, and receiving on board the second detachment of Naval Brigade proceeded up the Hooghly with her jolly-boat in tow.

☾ *September* 21*st.*—Cutwa. This is the first station we have stopped at for coal: the town is situated at the point where the two rivers Bargarutti and Hadjee run into the Hooghly, the former of which we ascend to-morrow; we have come a hundred and twenty miles, and already find the weather cooler. Several passengers are going with us to Allahabad, amongst others the Rev. T. Moore, appointed chaplain of Cawnpore, Colonel Longden of H. M. 10th Regiment, and Captain Maxwell of the Bengal Artillery.

♀ *September* 25*th.*—We are now above Berhampore where the steamer River Bird is on shore; we tried to tug her off, but in vain, so they will have to wait for the dry season, and then make a regular dock for her, as she is only about fifteen feet from the channel.

Captain Peel only went as far as Berhampore in the Chunar; here her engines proved so defective that he applied for another steamer, and the River Bird was sent to him: she went up as far as Dinapore, when it was found that she drew too much water to proceed any further: Captain Peel then went on in the steamer Mirzapore, which finally brought the flat up to Allahabad. The River Bird got on shore on her way down to Calcutta.

♄ *September* 26*th.*—Above Berhampore. The day before yesterday, we saw a faint blue line rising above the horizon, and since then the Rajmahal range of hills has gradually risen to view: it is quite a novelty to be in a country so flat that one can uninterruptedly mark the approach to hills from a great distance: some of the green jungle scenery on the banks of the river is pretty: the current here is very strong, and we have been struggling with it all day.

☉ *September* 27*th.*—We hear that the steamer Chunar, with Captain Sotheby of the Pearl on board, has stuck in the mud, and is now about twenty miles ahead of us; however, we hope that our good boat, the Benares, will take us all the way up to Allahabad without accident, as she draws less water.

♂ *September* 29*th.*—We have been steaming along all day, as usual, and are now close to the Rajmahal hills, which are very pretty after the flat country through which we have been passing for so long:

they are partly covered with woods, of which the trees are much less tall than those on the plains; the Ganges here attains its greatest size and strength, and the current is very powerful: there does not appear to be much cultivation, at any rate near the banks of the river; a few huts are to be seen, the natives being chiefly engaged in pastoral occupations. There is a remarkable race of Highlanders called the "Sonthals," who live amongst the wilds of the Rajmahal hills; they are very fierce, powerful, and athletic, they have never been subdued, and sometimes make incursions from their mountain fastnesses upon the helpless Hindoos. We just touched on a mud-bank this morning, but on the whole are making a good passage, wonderfully free from accidents, if not very rapid. In the forenoon we assisted an E. I. C. gun-boat which we found with both her anchors stuck fast in the mud.

☿ *September 30th.*—We are now a little way below three rocks in the middle of the Ganges, called the Colgong rocks; they rise to the height of fifty or sixty feet from the water, and are much rent and torn, and in their ragged clefts grow most picturesque trees and shrubs; it is not very easy to pass these rocks as the current is so strong. We pass our days very pleasantly: in the morning at daylight we heave the anchor up, and as soon as we are fairly under weigh, all hands fall in for an hour's drill: then follows breakfast, and at about nine parade, with perhaps a quarter of an hour's drill: by this time it is too hot to do much, so the day is spent in reading and writing, listening to the sonorous but rather wearisome chant of the native leadsman, "tien barmi lâni," and shooting at birds and alligators until 5 P.M., when we have another parade and about half an hour's drill; at six we dine, at sunset we anchor, and the evening is passed under the awning in reading, singing, and other amusements.

♄ *October 3rd.*—Jehangeerah. Yesterday morning we landed all our men at Bhagulpore for drill. The

JEHANGEERAH.

river here is seven miles broad, and we are now steaming along with flat country on the starboard and hilly country on the port side.

☉ *October 4th.*—Above Monghir. This morning we arrived at Monghir, and left again in the afternoon: it is a very pretty town surrounded by a semi-ruinous wall built by the Hindoos about a hundred years ago, when this place marked the British frontier: it is protected by a fort of great antiquity, built on a picturesque site on a rock jutting out into the river. The town wall is of very great extent, and encloses a space said to be larger than Fort William at Calcutta. This place is remarkable for the number of wooden folding-chairs made in it; also for its hammers with iron handles, which unscrew and disclose a knife, fork, and corkscrew, ingeniously but roughly made; also for small mats and hand-punkahs made of a particular sort of grass. Here also are manufactured guns and rifles, bearing the names of celebrated English gunsmiths, and so skilfully imitated that one would not at first sight detect the deception; those, however, who are allured by their cheapness into buying them, generally find that bullets fired from them possess very erratic propensities, and they frequently burst after a few discharges. The country to the south of the Ganges still maintains its hilly character, while that to the north is flat and muddy. To-day has been set apart by the Governor-General, as a day of humiliation and prayer, and a fund is to be raised for the benefit of the wives and families of those who may fall in quelling the mutiny.

October 6th.—This morning, just before noon, our steamer grounded; it was the first time since leaving Calcutta, so that, on the whole, we may consider ourselves rather fortunate: it was 9 P.M. before we get her off, though our men worked hard all day, assisting the steamer's crew.

☿ *October* 7*th.*—Twelve days hence we hope to reach Allahabad; the weather is already much cooler.

♄ *October* 10*th.*—Yesterday afternoon we left the large military station of Dinapore, taking with us two small field-pieces for Captain Sotheby at Buxar. Dinapore seems to be the most civilised place that we have touched at on our journey from Calcutta: we heard there that Delhi was taken, its king captured, and his two sons shot; we heard also of the relief of Lucknow and death of General Neil; and that Captain Peel has arrived safely at Allahabad with all his men and guns. The hills that we used to see to the southward and eastward have disappeared; the country is flat on both sides, and the water very muddy, but the river not so broad. We pass many dead bodies, in various stages of decomposition, floating down the river; they are generally the bodies of natives which have been partly burnt on the banks of the sacred Ganges, and are sometimes brought from a considerable distance for this purpose, by their affectionate relatives: when the families are too poor to afford a funeral pyre, the body is simply cast into the water, food for the crows and vultures. Every day we have several hours hard drill; we landed all hands twice at Dinapore, and we find that our men do very well at the manual and platoon exercises, at which they are of course well drilled on board, but they make occasional mistakes in marching and wheeling, for which there is not space on the deck of the flat. Perhaps the most difficult thing for sailors to learn is to keep such a distance when marching in file that they will fall into their right places in fronting. We never insist much on their keeping step; this will come in time.

When I was writing yesterday evening, an enormous locust with large wings, swooped down upon my desk, the wings then suddenly disappeared, and the creature began hopping about the table on its spider-like legs in a most grotesque manner. I threw my handkerchief over him and popped him into a bottle of gin; I examined him when he was dead, and found him to be of about the size of a small bat, but having the power of shutting up his large transparent wings into a kind of tape, and then rolling them up into a ball on the hinder part of his back; hence their sudden disappearance. I caught another shortly afterwards, and now they are both in a pickle bottle full of gin, ready to send down to the Shannon by the first opportunity.

☉ *October* 11*th.*—Above Dinapore. The evenings now begin to get very cool, and last night so cold that I was glad of a blanket; but the days are still warm, the sun hot and the winds cool. We are beginning to make better progress; the current is not so strong above Dinapore, as there are fewer tributaries; we hope to reach Allahabad in about ten days, and very glad shall we be to rejoin our old shipmates.

☽ *October* 12*th.*—Yesterday evening we arrived at Buxar, where we saw Captain Sotheby and his party; it is an old mud fort, built by the Hindoos; its chief strength consists in a very deep ditch by which it is surrounded, crossed in one place by a narrow drawbridge. There are at present only five or six small brass guns, but if there were a dozen larger ones it would be rather a strong place, and resist a considerable body of Sepoys. The men and officers of the Pearl are all letting their beards and moustaches grow, but Captain Peel has given an order that his Naval Brigade are to continue to shave; however, we are not very particular about the beards.

♂ *October* 13*th.*—Ten miles below Ghazeepore. A bar of sand here crosses the river, which is actually fordable; over this bar we are forcing our way, although there is only about four foot of water, and we draw four foot six. It is a most unusual occurrence for the river to be so broad and so shallow; in a short time it will have formed for itself a channel; just at present it spreads over a breadth of perhaps two miles; but the rains are now over, and the waters have fallen.

☿ *October* 14*th.*—This Ganges is a wonderful river, its gigantic tributary streams, together with its own vast length through lands so fertile, and by cities so populous, ought to make India one of the first countries in the world. With reference to some remarks made in the House of Commons, suggesting that gun-boats should be sent out here for the protection of towns situated on the rivers, I believe that they would be invaluable; the gun-boats which were used in the last war mostly drew six or seven feet water; now I learn from Captain Elder who commands this steamer, a most intelligent and superior man, that for a gun-boat to be serviceable on the Ganges between Calcutta and Allahabad, in the dry season, she must not draw more water than two foot six; and for a gun-boat to be serviceable between Calcutta and Dinapore only, she must not draw more than four foot six. In the rainy season, a vessel drawing ten foot of water might go up as high as Allahabad, but in the dry season, a vessel drawing only two foot six when loaded with provisions, guns, coal, &c., would find some difficulty in getting up, although by heaving her over the mud, it might be done at all times of the year. Though the Ganges is so very shallow, there is generally plenty of breadth, so that gun-boats might be constructed of great beam, thirty feet at least, to enable them to draw so little water. There are many depôts of coal along the river, so that a gun-boat would not require to have great stowage of fuel. The East India Company has a sort of gun-raft consisting of two boats decked over with a large paddle-wheel between them; this raft draws three foot water, and carries four 12-pr. brass howitzers; surely this might be improved upon. It would not be a very great objection to gun-boats for the Ganges to have the engines above water-line; even if they *were* damaged in action, they might be rowed or even punted with poles in shallow water, where the current does not run too strong; in smooth water like the Ganges, an engagement would be quite a different thing to one on the open sea, where damage to the engines might be attended by the total loss of the boat. Last night we reached Ghazeepore, where we found H.M.'s 37th Regiment; it seems to be a large, straggling station with plenty of trees and open ground, and is notoriously healthy. We saw some Hindoos burning a body as we passed to-day, the odour from which was very sickening. The river here is much narrower, but the country does not appear as if it was much flooded during the heavy rains; no hills are to be seen in any direction. The natives are very much surprised at the continuous flood of soldiers that are arriving, and want to know where they all come from; it is to be hoped it will produce a good moral effect on them. To-morrow forenoon we hope to arrive at Benares. One man, who is now recovering from cholera, is the only serious case of illness that we have had since we left Calcutta, although many men are on the sick list with boils and sores from inflamed musquito bites.

♀ *October* 16*th*.—Last night we arrived at Benares, the Oxford of India and head-quarters of Sanscrit scholarship: it is a very large Hindoo city of great antiquity, on the north bank of the Ganges, with many curious old specimens of architecture: the view from the water is one of the finest of its kind in India, as the river bends first towards and then from it; the water side is lined with magnificent flights of broad stone steps called ghauts, which are the daily lounge of the native population; here they undergo the process of washing in the sacred river, which is fortunately a religious ceremony, and then sit on the steps, smoking, or dozing, or besmearing themselves with the marks of their caste in yellow paint or sacred Ganges mud. The houses of the native town are small, but there are numerous mosques, the peculiarly oriental gracefulness of whose swelling domes and tapering minarets attract and charm the eye, although in size they cannot compete with those of the head-quarters of Islamism: here, as at Stamboul, the town does not improve on acquaintance; one finds on landing only steep, narrow, and ill-paved streets which will afford passage to no wheeled vehicle. To-morrow we hope to arrive at Mirzapore.

♄ *October* 17*th*.—To-day we passed Chunar, one of the most picturesque fortresses in India, situated on a high sandstone rock on the south bank of the river, and completely commanding it: it is deservedly held in great estimation by the Hindoos, who have a tradition that it is under the direct protection of the Almighty, and cannot be captured: English troops took it by assault some years ago, but that has not shaken their faith in the least.

October 18th.—Yesterday at about 1·30 P.M. we arrived at Mirzapore, which we left early this morning: it is the last station before we reach Allahabad, and a principal commercial city. We have to-day met with such a strong current that we have been obliged to anchor, and to-morrow it will be as much as we shall be able to do to stem it. I brought a letter of introduction to Mr. Venables, a merchant here, who distinguished himself very much in the mutiny, and he was so good as to invite me to dine with him in the evening at his bungalow about a mile from the ghaut. Now a "ghaut" is a term applied equally to a mountain pass, or a landing-place; I believe that it means literally "a passage;" a "bungalow" is, properly speaking, "a summer country house;" most people in Bengal have offices and "go-downs" (storehouses) in town, and a bungalow in a "compound" a little way out of town. A "compound" is the enclosure in which a house is situated, and this one word includes what in England would be called a yard, a park, a shrubbery, or grounds. Mirzapore is a large town, situated on the frontiers of the rebellious country;

it is now garrisoned by a few Madras troops only, who openly say in the native bazaars that if the Sepoys come, they will join them: "for" say they, "what could we do? We are not strong enough to overcome them, and we should only be cut to pieces by our own countrymen if we resisted:" so the Europeans living there go to bed every night with the happy consciousness that they may all find their throats cut in the morning. From what I hear I believe that the natives of India do not, for the most part, side against us, except in Oude, where they bitterly hate us: there they are a very different race from the enervated Hindoo; they are bred to carry arms from their youth, and every one is a soldier from his childhood, both in feeling and carriage. We hear that the Sepoys have assembled near Lucknow, that there is a good deal of fighting going on, and that our troops find it as much as they can do to repel the attacks: but reinforcements are daily pouring in, and I believe that the Naval Brigade is likely to be sent on immediately.

☽ *October* 19*th.*—This evening we have anchored where we are not more than ten miles from Allahabad in a direct line, but very much further by the river. We hope to arrive there to-morrow about mid-day.

♂ *October* 20*th.*—This morning we landed, about half a mile from the Fort of Allahabad; the first detachment come down to meet us, and we all marched up to barracks together with the band playing.

CHAP. III.

GARRISON DUTY AT ALLAHABAD. — RELIEF OF LUCKNOW. — ENGAGEMENTS AT CAWNPORE.

☿ *October* 21*st.* — To-day we have been busily employed bringing the tents and baggage up from the steamer Benares.

♃ *October* 22*nd.* — To-morrow the advanced guard and siege-train, in charge of Lieut. Vaughan, with one hundred men and four officers, start for the front. The officers are, Lieut. Salmon, Mr. M. Daniel, Lords W. Kerr and A. Clinton, midshipmen: Mr. E. Daniel, who received the Victoria Cross when serving under Captain Peel in the Crimea, has already been sent on to Cawnpore, as an artillery officer was telegraphed for. We have got very good quarters here, and have turned regular soldiers; officers patrol all night and mount guard, and our men drill far better than we could have expected. We have five parades and two drills daily; at the morning parade it is quite a sight to see our men fall in under the colonnades of the barracks: each one puts on a clean suit of clothes from head to foot daily, there being a proportion of "dobies" (washermen) to each company; every man wears shoes, which are well blacked and polished; and the mountings of the Minié or Enfield rifles glisten in the sun: the officers fall in, and such drill as can be performed in the shade is gone through.

♄ *October* 24*th*.—Yesterday morning Lieut. Vaughan left with his detachment. Another party is now ordered to be ready to start, consisting of Lieuts. Young and Hay, Mr. Garvey, mate, and Mr. Church, midshipman. From what one hears of campaigning in India in time of peace, it seems to be generally little more than a pic-nic; tents are provided for the officers, lined with a sort of coarse, coloured chintz, carpeted, with blinds for the doors to keep the sun out. In peace-time, the march of a body of men averages twelve miles a day; and when they arrive at the end of their march, they find that the servants have pitched the tents, prepared a meal, and put out a change of linen; the "bheestie" is ready with a skin of water for a bath, and the dobie is waiting to wash the clothes they take off.

☿ *October* 28*th*.—6 A.M. Exercised at light infantry and company drill. 10 A.M. Mustered by companies. Cleared lower barracks of slops, stores, &c., and placed them in an upper room. At 1·30 P.M. the second company of the Naval Brigade, under the command of Lieut. Hay, marched out with Captain Peel: the officers accompanying them are, Mr. Bowman, chaplain; Mr. Garvey, mate; Mr. Church, midshipman; and Messrs. Watson and Lascelles, aides-de-camp to the Captain; besides these, he takes up two engineers, with the carpenter and artificers. There remain now to garrison this large fort about a hundred and fifty men of the Naval Brigade, including sick, band, and officers. The officers remaining behind are, Lieut. Wilson, in command; Lieut. Wratislaw, commanding the first company, whose subalterns are Mr. Way, midshipman, and myself; Mr. Lind, of Hageby, a lieutenant in the Swedish navy, doing duty as a mate in our service, commanding the third company, whose subaltern is Mr. Richards, naval cadet; Mr. Thompson, gunner; Mr. Comerford, assistant-paymaster; and Mr. Staunton, assistant-clerk. We expect to follow the others very shortly. Yesterday I was doing duty as subaltern of the main guard, and this morning I turned out the guard to salute Captain Peel and his party as they passed out.

♃ *October* 29*th.*—Sent ten men to hospital; total number of men sick, sixty-four. A fatigue-party of thirty men employed at the arsenal arranging stores; issued rifles to the band. Died in hospital, Henry Patt, bandsman. Seventeen officers and two hundred and sixty-seven men marched into barracks on the strength of the garrison.

♀ *October* 30*th.*—Forty coolies employed hauling up the jolly-boat and cutter. The fortress of Allahabad is situated in the fork made by the confluence of the Rivers Ganges and Jumna, and has always been regarded as a very strong and important military post; it can accommodate a large number of men in tents, but only six hundred in the barracks; it was built about two hundred years ago, but the land face has since been considerably modernised; the two river faces have not been much altered, and consist of imposing walls and massive bastions of red sandstone, pierced with the small embrasures and loopholes characteristic of the old days of Oriental chivalry; the fort contains the largest arsenal in this part of India: it is entered by three approaches, the Main, the Jumna, and the Ganges Gates,—the latter of these is bricked up, and no longer used, but the Main Gate, approached through the winding ways of modern fortification, is a handsome entrance, on each side of which are cells, reserved for State prisoners in close confinement. About five hundred yards from the glacis, a permanent camp has been pitched, for the use of regiments passing up the country; near the fort is the town of Allahabad proper, which consists almost entirely of native huts; about two miles to the eastward of it are the cantonments, which were formerly the prettiest in this part of India; now only a few of the houses are habitable, and the rest are but half burnt ruins, looking most desolate in their deserted and abandoned gardens; the church too has been sacked and burned, but could be restored; the roads near the cantonments are very good, and the country is prettily wooded.

♄ *October* 31*st.*—4·30 A.M. Sent a fatigue-party of twenty men to the railway station to transport camel carts. Carpenters employed painting boats. Launched cutter to send for Lieut.-General Sir Colin Campbell, K.C.B., Commander-in-Chief. 9 P.M. Sent an escort of one officer and twenty-one men to meet Sir Colin Campbell at the bridge of boats over the Ganges. Sixty-seven men in hospital. On this day, the detachment of the Naval Brigade under Sir William Peel arrived at Futtehpore.

☉ *November* 1*st.*—3 A.M. Sir Colin Campbell and suite arrived; and at sunrise the garrison fired a salute of seventeen guns. 10 A.M. Mustered by companies, and performed Divine service. Number of sick, seventy.

☽ *November* 2*nd.*—7·30 A.M. Sir Colin Campbell and suite left the garrison, under a salute of seventeen guns. Exercised the band at rifle drill. Number of sick, sixty-three.

♂ *November* 3*rd.*—A company of H.M. 82nd Regiment marched into barracks. Number of sick, sixty-one. To-day we have heard of Captain Peel's engagement at Kudjwa, the following brief account of which is from the pen of our chaplain, Mr. Bowman:—

☉ *November* 1*st.*—5·30 A.M. A force consisting of a hundred men and officers of the Naval Brigade, with Lieut.

Hay, Mr. Garvey, Lieut. Stirling, R.M., and Mr. Bone, one company of Royal Engineers, two companies of H. M. 53rd Regiment, and a detachment of sixty men of different regiments, afterwards joined by one company of H. M. 90th Highlanders, about five hundred and thirty men in all, the whole under command of Colonel Powell, C.B., started from Futtehpore in pursuit of a body of the mutineers: after marching twenty-four miles, at 3 P.M. they came within sight of the enemy, found them intrenched in a strong position behind some hillocks of sand, and driving their skirmishers out of a field of long corn, engaged and defeated them, capturing two guns and an ammunition waggon: the whole force of the enemy exceeded four thousand men, of whom about two thousand were Sepoys and fought in uniform, many with medals on their breasts. Their loss in the action was estimated at over four hundred killed, and included their commander and wounded. Colonel Powell was killed early in the action, when the command devolved on Captain Peel. The battle was fought near the village of Kudjwa, and lasted two hours and a half, the force encamping in the vicinity of a village called Binkee that evening. The following day, the force under Captain Peel returned to Futtehpore in high spirits, and was received with loud cheering. Lieut. Hay, R.N. was slightly wounded in the hand, and Lieut. Stirling, R.M. was severely wounded in the calf of the leg.*

☿ *November 4th.*—A company of H.M. 82nd Regiment marched into barracks.

♀ *November 6th.*—9·30 P.M. Lieut. Wratislaw, with fifty men, left the garrison, by order of Brigadier Campbell, to protect the hospital. Some men were seen prowling round the walls of the fort the other

* See Appendix.

night, and the Brigadier ordered me out with a picquet to see what they were about; the men ran away, but our attention was thus drawn to some windows in the wall, open drains, and the arsenal, all of which were in a very unprotected state. As this fortress is not strongly garrisoned, great precautions are taken both by day and night; after gun-fire, the drawbridges are hauled up, and the gates locked, and there is neither ingress nor egress without written permission from the commandant; all the sentries are visited, guards turned out, and walls patrolled twice during the night, by the subaltern commanding the main guard, and once by the captain of the week; any person within or without the fort not answering when hailed, is fired at by the sentry, and on hearing a shot fired all the guards turn out. Some years ago, a very curious pillar, some fifty feet long, was found here, made of one solid piece of stone; the colonel then commanding the garrison had it set up in the middle of the parade-ground, with a comical-looking carved lion on the top. It goes by the name of Bheem Singh's Lat. A Calcutta Magazine gives the following account of it: "It is one stone, 42 feet 7 inches in height, of which 7 feet 7 inches may be considered the base, which was probably buried to some extent in the ground, or in the masonry that supported it. The shaft, properly so called, is 3 feet in diameter at the base, diminishing to 2 feet 2 inches at the summit; the neck, immediately below the capital, represents with considerable purity the honeysuckle ornament of the Assyrians, which the Greeks borrowed from them with the Ionic order. The pillar at Allahabad lost its capital, but the deficiency was supplied from two of the Tirhoot examples which retain their capitals, with the lions which crowned the summits of all. This pillar is one of a group of monolites set up by Asoka in the middle of the third century, B.C.; they were all alike in form, and all bore the same inscription, being four short edicts, containing the creed and principal doctrines of Bhuddism, which he had recently embraced. Of these one is at Delhi, having been re-erected by Feroze-shah in his palace, as a monument of his victory over the Hindoos; three more are standing near the River Gunduck, in Tirhoot; a fragment of another was discovered near Delhi, and part of a seventh was used as a roller on the Benares road by a Company's engineer officer." On this day, Captain Peel, with the first detachment of the Naval Brigade, arrived at Cawnpore.

♄ *November 7th.*—6·30 A.M. Lieut. Wratislaw and party returned from the hospital. H. M. 82nd Regiment marched out of barracks. Carpenters employed painting boats. Died, Michael Shea, R.M. By order of the commandant, Brigadier Campbell, porter is now served out to our men.

☉ *November 8th.*—6·30 A.M. Mustered by companies and marched to the garrison chapel. 5 P.M. Sent funeral party to inter the remains of Michael Shea, deceased. Number of sick, sixty-four.

♃ *November* 12*th.*—The following account of the operations of the detachment of the Naval Brigade which accompanied Sir Colin Campbell to the relief of Lucknow, is from the journal of our chaplain: a list of the officers will be found in the last chapter.

> ♃ *November* 12*th.*—The Naval Brigade arrived at the camping ground near the Alumbagh; a short time before their arrival, about two thousand of the enemy were observed on the left, about a thousand yards off, among corn and sugar-cane fields; our men immediately brought their great guns into position on the road, and the Horse Artillery, Highlanders and Lancers went in pursuit; after firing a few round shot, the enemy dispersed.

♀ *November* 13*th.*—Last night, the wounded from the battle of Kudjwa arrived, and amongst them were Lieut. Stirling, R.M. and an officer of the 93rd of the name of Conyngham; both were wounded by a bullet in the calf of the leg.

♄ *November* 14*th.*—The washermen knock our clothes to pieces terribly, but get them beautifully white and clean, far beyond anything I ever saw in England; this, however, is chiefly owing to the burning sun, which would bleach a chimney-sweep in about ten minutes, brushes and all. Our men have all sorts of pets: cats, dogs, goats, pigeons, monkeys, parrots, and even sheep and squirrels; every morning, about twenty men and monkeys go down to a covered bath in the ditch of the fort, adjoining which is a smaller one used by the officers. Every barrack-room has a small square hole in each of its four corners for ventilation, and what with the birds flying in at the windows and out through the ceiling, one's room is a perfect aviary.

♄ *November* 14*th.*—(From Mr. Bowman's Journal.) The whole force got under weigh, and proceeded by a circuitous route to attack Lucknow; on the march, which was among cornfields and woods that would have afforded splendid cover for the enemy, the troops were several times engaged, and on one occasion some of the Highlanders were driven back, but being reinforced, compelled the enemy to retreat: on nearing Lucknow they made a stand, but were driven back with the loss of two guns. Two large buildings, or rather palaces were taken by our troops; one, called the Dilkushah, is a royal hunting-seat, situated on a hill overlooking Lucknow; the other, a European college called the Martinière, built by a Frenchman, General Martine, who was commander-in-chief of the Oude army many years ago, is situated a little below the Dilkushah. We now all moved into a compound near the Martinière, but had hardly occupied it when several round shot were fired right among us; at the same time a determined attack was made by the enemy with musketry, which soon obliged us all, men and guns, to evacuate the place. Our large guns were rapidly taken, under a heavy fire, into a position whence they might drive back the enemy, and some troops were also ordered to charge, the enemy were repulsed, and we then returned and bivouacked for the night. We had a sad misfortune with one of our guns; it accidentally went off while being loaded, probably on account of not having been properly sponged, killed Francis Cassiday, captain of the maintop, severely wounded two other blue jackets, killed one Highlander, and severely wounded two others. The total loss of the army to-day has been upwards of twenty killed and wounded, and among the former are two officers of the Carabineers.

⊙ *November* 15*th.*—(From Mr. Bowman's Journal.) The army rested.

☽ *November* 16*th.*—(From Mr. Bowman's Journal.) The 8th Regiment, Hodson's horse, and three guns of the Royal Artillery, under command of Lieut. Walker, the whole under command of Colonel Little, remained at the Dilkushah to guard the baggage, stores, sick and wounded: the remainder of the army proceeded to attack Lucknow. Presently the advanced guard was heard in conflict with the enemy; when the Naval Brigade guns came up to where the fighting was going on, they found that a sort of summer palace called the Secundra Bagh, was being attacked: it was full of Sepoys, who kept up a killing fire from the roofs and neighbouring walls. The engagement was very severe, and an officer came rushing back along the line shouting for infantry, and hurrying up the heavy guns. When the field hospital arrived at the scene of action, it took up its position under the walls of the Secundra Bagh, inside of which the fighting was still going on: this was the safest position that could be selected, but the shot, shell, and musket-balls were cutting the trees about in all directions, and falling among the wounded who were brought in rapidly; in a few hours the place was covered with doolies full of wounded, who were afterwards removed to beds placed along the wall. In the evening a report was spread that one of the adjacent towers contained a magazine; this caused a panic, and the whole of the wounded were removed into the open, where they remained for some time: afterwards the report was found to have been false; they were moved back again, and there they remained during the first awful night. Lieut. Salmon was brought in, wounded in the thigh by a musket-ball during the afternoon. Martin Abbot Daniel, midshipman, was killed by a round shot which tore away the right side of his head. In writing to his father, Captain Peel says: "It was in the front of the Shah Najeef, and in command of an 8-in. howitzer, that your noble son was killed; the enemy's fire was very heavy, and I had just asked your son if his gun was ready; he replied "All ready, sir," when I said, "Fire the howitzer," and he was answering "Aye, aye," when a round shot in less than a moment deprived him of life. We buried him where he fell, our chaplain reading the service, and in laying him in his resting place we felt, captain, officers and men, that we had lost one of the best and noblest of the Shannons." The firing slackened considerably during the night, and our troops advanced some distance towards the Residency, having stormed and taken the barracks and several bungalows. Twelve or thirteen of the Naval Brigade were brought in wounded, and three or four were killed.

November 17*th.*—(From Mr. Bowman's Journal.) On account of the unsafe position and exposed situation of the hospital, the sick were removed this morning to a village about a hundred and fifty yards off: this village was built, as are many in Oude, consisting of a square court, surrounded by mud cottages, whose doors and windows all open to the interior: on the outside are very thick blank mud walls, the whole forming rather a strong fortification. The sick had not been here long before the enemy had evidently received information of the move, for several round shot were sent into the court, the second of which killed two camels which were lying down in the centre of the square, the third going right through the roof of the building in which Dr. Dickson and some of the staff were living. The hospital was in a most precarious position, as it was open to the rear, a large breach having been made in the wall, and no sentries having been posted at the entry. During the night heavy firing was heard close to, probably the enemy engaging our picquets: a few men coming in might have massacred the whole of our sick and wounded; but the night passed without any attempt being made, although a general attack was expected, the bells ringing every half hour and the firing recommencing each time. To-day, great cheering was heard all round, which announced the fact that communication had been opened with the Residency. Generals Havelock and Outram met Sir Colin Campbell, and the women and children were now considered out of danger.

♀ *November 20th.*—The garrison saluted Major-General Dupuis, R.A., with thirteen guns, on his leaving the fort. This evening we received intelligence that there were two thousand Sepoys about three miles off: all the troops in the permanent camp were immediately got under arms, and everyone in the fort was on the "qui-vive"; but there was no attack, and all ended in smoke. A few nights ago, we sent out an advanced picquet of fifty men, and on another occasion, two field-pieces and a hundred men, but neither time did any Sepoys appear; so either spies must have brought false intelligence, or the rebels taken alarm.

☾ *November 23rd.*—(From Mr. Bowman's Journal.) Last night, the whole force retreated from Lucknow, and arrived at the Dilkushah. The retrogade movement was made in a most successful manner, without any pursuit or annoyance from the enemy. A large number of shot were necessarily left behind in the Residency, and also a few disabled guns.

♂ *November 24th.*—(From Mr. Bowman's Journal.) The army started from the Dilkushah for the Alumbagh, leaving behind two of the Naval Brigade guns and two thousand men to cover the retreat, and follow on the succeeding day. General Havelock died this day at the Dilkushah, of dysentery: he will be buried to-morrow in the Alumbagh. A 24-pr. about a thousand yards off annoys the garrison of the Alumbagh very much, several shots having struck the tents, and a few natives having been killed: this gun goes by the name of "Nancy Dawson." The Sepoy commanders pay their men for every round shot or bullet they bring in: this affords very pretty practice for our picquets, as there are constantly several men out in the open, picking up shot that fall short.

♃ *November* 26*th.*—Allahabad contains many valuable stores and is very strong, yet it has no standing garrison besides the Naval Brigade. I have had my room partitioned off with grass mats, to keep out the draughts; there is no sort of protection in these barracks from cold in winter, nothing has been thought of but how to keep them cool in summer. We hear that there is a party of Sepoys between Cawnpore and Lucknow intercepting the post, which may account for our receiving no news from that direction.

♄ *November* 28*th.*—(From Mr. Bowman's Journal.) Orders arrived early in the morning for the Naval Brigade to march at 7 A.M. Captain Peel took upon himself to ignore the order, and directed the men to get their breakfasts before starting; at noon they marched fifteen miles, and then received orders to bivouac for two hours, after this they again started and reached the camp of the main army, about three miles from Cawnpore, at 2 A.M. No tents were pitched, but the guns were kept ready for action. We hear that the Gwalior Contingent attacked Cawnpore on the 26th, and

General Wyndham hearing that they were approaching, went out to meet them with about fifteen hundred men: they fell in with a strong reconnoitring party of the enemy, attacked and defeated them, capturing three guns; they then returned and encamped about two miles from Cawn pore: the next day at 11·30 A.M. the alarm was sounded, and thirty-six blue jackets with two 24-prs. with Mr. Garvey, mate, under command of Lieut. Hay, advanced to meet the enemy, and after a short time came in sight of them. The enemy fired the first shot from a gun on the road, but as soon as our guns replied, they opened fire with grape and canister from batteries on either side of it: our guns not being properly supported, and being in advance of the skirmishers, Lieut. Hay received orders from General Dupuis to retire and leave them, which he did, having spiked one: our blue jackets advanced again shortly afterwards with the Rifles and 88th, and brought them in: Lieut. Hay was struck in the stomach by a spent grape-shot, and carried to the rear. The retreat now became general, and our troops pursued by the enemy and harassed by musketry, reached the entrenched camp at about 5·30 P.M. with their guns. Mr. H. A. Lascelles, naval cadet, A.D.C. to Captain Peel, distinguished himself a good deal, seizing a rifle from a wounded man of the 88th, and charging with that regiment.

☾ *November* 30*th*.—We were all much astonished this morning to see a post-captain in top-boots, spurs, and corduroys, come riding across the parade-ground; he wore a full-dress sword-belt, and a curious looking sword, very much curved, and broad, with a wooden hilt, an undress frock-coat with the three stripes, and a number of shiny leather accoutrements hanging about him by marvellously contrived straps; there was a drinking flask, a revolver case, a present-use pouch, a reserve pouch, and a telescope case, all made of black shiny leather; his saddle was quite new and white, with white holsters and bags hanging from it, white bridle, and white reins; this all turned out to be Captain Oliver Jones, an officer on half-pay, come up here for a *lark* as he told me.

CHAP. IV.

MARCH TO CAWNPORE. RECAPTURE OF CAWNPORE. — THE "YELLOW BUNGALOW."

☉ *December 6th.*—8·30 A.M. Received orders per electric telegraph for Lieut. Wilson, Mr. Verney, the band, and eighty men to proceed to Cawnpore.

☾ *December 7th.* — Cheemee. Yesterday, at three hours' notice, we left Allahabad for Cawnpore. Since Captain Peel started, one thought has been uppermost in each mind, namely, the desire to follow him. When we left yesterday, the scene among our men ordered to remain was most extraordinary, old petty-officers and young seamen giving way to floods of tears at not being ordered to the front. This is the end of the railway at present, and we march this afternoon at one or two o'clock with bullock-waggons. We have just met Lieuts. Hay and Salmon going to Allahabad wounded, with the women, children, and wounded relieved from Lucknow: Lieut. Salmon is shot through the thigh, and Lieut. Hay has received an internal wound, caused by a spent ball striking his sword-belt; Lieuts. Young and Salmon have been recommended for the Victoria Cross. I hear that at Cawnpore shot and shell are flying into the tents. Lieut. Young is at present in command of our men at that place.

Futtehpore. We hear that the road between this and Cawnpore is not safe, but that the rebels have been well thrashed. Our journey, even this far, has been full of adventures, an account of which in an idle moment (see April 22nd, 1858) might amuse; but as they chiefly consisted of carts breaking down, and oxen and waggons weaving themselves into a curious and writhing fabric.

(From Mr. Bowman's Journal.) Orders have come for the baggage to proceed immediately to the Commander-in-Chief's camp, about three miles off on the Calpee Road. The enemy deserted the city of Cawnpore at about three o'clock this morning; yesterday they had guns in position to play upon the Grand Trunk Road; when our guns went to attack them they appeared taken by surprise, and did not at first return the fire. After encountering rather a heavy fire for a short time, they retreated with our men full in pursuit. They made one stand behind an entrenchment, which was stormed and carried by the Royal Marines under Captain Gray, R.M., and the 53rd. The enemy then fled down the Calpee Road, pursued by our troops, that being the only one open to them, as a two-gun battery commanded by Lord Walter Kerr was opposed to them on the Futtehpore Road. Seventeen guns were captured, also their camp, which contained a great portion of the things taken from the 88th, 90th, &c., on the occasion of General Wyndham's retreat. The cavalry pursued the enemy for about fifteen miles, cutting them to pieces, and our guns went down the road about nine miles: in the evening the troops returned with a great quantity of baggage and ammunition. Our loss has been very trifling; two officers were killed — Lieut. Vincent of the 8th, and Lieut. Salmond of the Staff; the latter was found with his throat cut, a short distance down the Calpee Road. The loss of the Naval Brigade was two men slightly wounded.

KERR'S BATTERY. CAWNPORE.

☿ *December* 9*th.* — Futtehpore. This day at noon we start; four of our men who were ordered to remain behind have smuggled themselves into our party. Yesterday we caught a Sepoy with a large quantity of spoil, amongst which was a pair of cymbals, which the chief magistrate of the place kindly gave us, and they will be a great addition to our band.

♃ *December* 10*th.* — Alas! we are detained at Futtehpore; however, there is no fighting going on now at Cawnpore, so matters might be much worse. This place is distant from Allahabad seventy miles, and from Cawnpore fifty.

☉ *December* 13*th.*—Cawnpore. We marched in here yesterday at noon; on the road I purchased a bottle of brandy for one pound, thinking myself most fortunate in being able to do so: not half an hour afterwards Captain Oliver Jones rode up and presented me with another bottle; I do not remember to have ever received a more valuable present, or one for which I felt more gratitude. Now we have arrived we find that there are not tents for us, so we sleep in the tents of those who were here before, and spend the greater part of our time in the open air. Although I know that the opinion is not generally entertained, I give the result of my own short experience when I say that I find the natives of India tractable, and the better classes, such as servants, &c., grateful and honest. The English residents generally appear to me very prejudiced against the natives, and show this in their behaviour; for my own part, I must say that I receive many marks of attachment from my servants, in return for the trifling acts of kindness which I endeavour to do them. Contrary to the advice which was given me, I have treated my kitmagar kindly, and have reposed confidence in him; I try to gain his good-will, and he has amply repaid me by following me up here when he had a very bad foot; he said that I was a good master, and he knew I depended on his coming up, and would not disappoint me. As for the abject tillers of the soil, I fear they are so stupid, so ignorant, so wanting in the characteristics which distinguish the man from the brute, that I could quite understand instinct leading them to murder a sleeping man for the sake of the piece of bread in his hand. I think that a cause of the mutiny *may* be that in every British mind in India contempt for the natives is deeply rooted. When a kindness is done to a native by an Englishman, it is often accompanied by a contemptuous thought which appears only too clearly in the countenance; the terms in which I have heard even clergymen and others, who would desire to do good to the Hindoos, speak of them, convinces me that this is the case; it must be most trying to a people who consider us as outcasts.

☾ *December* 14*th.*—To-day we have shifted camp to a plain two miles further from Cawnpore.

♂ *December* 15*th.*—Lieut. Vaughan and Lord Walter Kerr have started with a party of blue jackets for Bithoor, where Nanà Sahib had his palace: they are gone to assist in pumping out some wells, at the bottom of which treasure is said to lie, as a silver cup was fished out of one with a spear.

♀ *December* 18*th.*—Lieut. Vaughan returned with his party, but had been unsuccessful in making any head against the springs supplying the wells at Bithoor.

☉ *December* 20*th.*—We are now encamped about three miles from Cawnpore. Ever since our arrival I have suffered from extreme lassitude attended with weakness, giddiness, and loss appetite, which renders me totally unequal to any exertion of mind or body, although up to the present time my name has not appeared on the sick list. I have been taking a mixture of quinine which has done me much good, and I hope it may now please God that I may recover. We have two pieces of news this morning; one is that all the rest of the Naval Brigade are coming up from Allahabad; the other that a large force of the rebels, with fifteen guns, refused to believe that Delhi had fallen, and advanced towards it; the British officer in command came out to meet them, utterly routed them and captured the fifteen guns. The chaplain here, the Rev. T. Moore, who came up with us in the "Benares" to Allahabad is the most hard-working man possible: hospitable and generous almost to excess, he spends a great portion of his time, often twelve hours out of the twenty-four, among the sick in the hospitals: he is at present laid up from over-work, but I trust will be about again in a day or two: he has hired a large house which, with the exception of one room, he has turned into a private hospital for wounded officers: under fire he has proved himself among the coolest and the bravest; he is a man of about five and thirty, although he looks ten years younger.

December 22nd.—Lieut. Wratislaw arrived at Cawnpore with the last detachment of the Naval Brigade. We have a most facetious petty officer of the name of Devereux; he is a good seaman but given to talking very bad *French;* one day on the passage out, when apostrophising the afterguard with even less politeness than usual, Captain Peel overheard him, and knowing him for an old offender turned sharply round on him; "What's that you say, sir?" said the Captain;

the man looked up scratching his old red head, with a knowing look on his scarred and wrinkled face, and with a sly twinkle in his eye replied: "I was making the remark, sir, as 'ow it blows werry 'ard in the Chiny seas." Of course this has now passed into a proverb among the Shannons.

☿ *December* 23*rd.*—7 A.M. Exercised the Naval Brigade together for the first time at company drill. 4 P.M. Exercised the first company at Light Infantry drill. A day or two ago I visited the "Yellow Bungalow," the house in which the barbarous massacres were committed; it is built in the form of a court; in the centre stands a tree, and all round is a verandah; I saw one of the rooms with its floors and walls covered with blood, although attempts had been made to whitewash the stains; from the beams of the verandah hung pieces of cord by which the children had been hung up, and stabbed by the Sepoys: on the wall behind a door was written with a pin or some sharp instrument, "Countrymen and women, remember 15 July, 1857. Your wives and families are here in misery, and at the disposal of savages who has ravished both old and young, and then killed us; oh! oh! my child, my child! countrymen revenge it." Near the house is the well into which the murdered bodies were thrown, and which has since been filled up.

CHAP. V.

MARCH FROM CAWNPORE TO FUTTEGURH. — CAMELS AND ELEPHANTS. — KUNNOJ. — ON THE LINE OF MARCH. — BATTLE OF THE KALLEE-NUDDEE.

♃ *December* 24*th.* — 6 A.M. Struck tents, and proceeded towards Futtegurh on the Grand Trunk Road. 1·30 P.M. Encamped, having marched thirteen miles.

♀ *December* 25*th.* — Christmas Day. 8·30 A.M. General parade; performed divine service. We are now sixteen or seventeen miles from Cawnpore, where we have left seventy-eight men and Lord Arthur Clinton, under the command of Lord Walter Kerr, midshipman. I soon got knocked up yesterday, as we marched until nearly noon, and it was one before the tents were pitched; but my syce led my horse by my side, and I rode at least four or five miles. We chummed together for our Christmas dinners, in parties of five or six, each bringing what he could to the general stock, and so we spent as merry a day as possible under the circumstances. Captain Peel has presented to the Commander-in-Chief, in the name of the Naval Brigade, as a Christmas present, a small brass cohorn, captured at Lucknow; it is mounted on a little carriage, with a suitable inscription, made by our engineers, assisted by the carpenters and stokers. Our engineers, Mr. Bone and Mr. Henri, have been of the greatest possible service, sighting our guns as accurately as rifles, and most zealously giving their whole energies to promoting the efficiency of our battery.

December 27*th.*—I have marched to-day the whole distance without mounting my horse; our march was only thirteen miles, so that an old stager would laugh at my considering it an achievement; but I do not think I could have marched much further. It is Sunday, but marching every day, it is difficult to make a difference between Sundays and week-days; there is the same routine of washing, feeding, and sleeping to be gone through, and it must be done on Sunday as well as on any other day. I find my horse most useful; he has such pluck that I know he would run as long as he could stand. To-day we have halted at a place called Arrown; and yesterday we encamped at Poorah, about twenty-six miles from Cawnpore. o morrow General Wyndham is to march with a strong brigade to a fort about eight miles off; if it is defended, he is to capture and blow it up. Lieut. Young and Mr. Daniel, midshipman, go in charge of a gun, which will be sent with two gun's crews. The country we are marching through is very flat, but generally well wooded, with a great deal of cultivation;

and the roads are good but dusty. Yesterday when we halted, a number of camels went to graze in a field of young wheat; the owner of the wheat came out, and called down curses from heaven on the camel-drivers; they were so appalled at this, that in three minutes they had driven out every camel: such is the effect of superstition. I fear that many of the camels are very badly used, as I sometimes see their backs bleeding when the pack-saddles are taken off. Young camels are frequently born on the march, and their mammas have to carry them for several days, until they are able to run pretty well; then a little wooden toggle is passed through the infant's nose, a piece of string connects it with the maternal tail, and thus it commences its walk through life, following in its parent's footsteps. A camel carries its supply of water in a large bladder; when thirsty, the animal has the power of bringing this up with a bubbling, gurgling sound, until it hangs down some eighteen inches below his mouth, and, having taken some of the water, he again swallows it; until one is accustomed to it, this is a most disagreeable and disgusting sight. When being laden he will give utterance to dismal moans, which become more piteous as his load increases; and if more is placed on his back than he approves of, he will start up, shake it all off and run "bobbery" through the camp, perhaps dragging after him, bumping and bounding over earth and stones, some valuable box, which has therefore been the more securely lashed to his pack-saddle. When unladen at night, he will sometimes frisk about with most grotesque antics; and surely, there is no more absurd sight in the world than a "larky" camel. To ride a camel is at first no easy matter; when you have climbed on to his hump, and laid hold of his pack-saddle, the "ont-wallah" gives the word, and the animal rises on his hind knees, with a "send" forward that will pitch the rider over his bows if he does not hold fast; before he has properly recovered his seat, the camel rises on his fore-feet, with a worse struggle than before, that threatens to send the rider flying over his stern; and a third "pitch" brings the camel on to all fours. But now commences a most trying discipline, for the beast begins to trot, and each step appears to dislocate every bone in your body, and it is only by practice that you learn to rise in the rope stirrups with each unexpected motion, so that at last the riding is even pleasant. The camel has large pad feet, whose natural cushion prevents this jarring from damaging the animal himself, and keeps his feet from sinking in soft sand: camels are at all times guided by a string attached to a wooden toggle passed through the nose, which in a caravan is fastened to his precursor's tail. At night, the camels of each regiment kneel down in a circle, their young ones and pack-saddles by their sides, their drivers in the centre, and thus they sleep on their stomachs:

many of them are very vicious, and if approached too closely by strangers, give a nasty tearing bite. The elephant is a far nobler and more intelligent creature; viewed as a piece of animal architecture, he is perhaps the most wonderful on earth. The largest of living creatures, his enormous proportions require corresponding support, which is found in his straight and massive legs; his arched back enables him to bear heavy burdens; and his strong head, set close on to his shoulders, enables him to concentrate his strength into a push. But the absence of a neck precludes him from putting his head to the ground, unless he kneels down, and therefore Providence has given him his marvellous trunk; with this he will pluck herbage from the ground, or tear down tender branches of trees for food; when directed he will pull down a house with it, root up a small tree, or chastise a bad brother; with this he drinks water; holding a branch in it he will fan away flies; or attacked by a tiger, with one blow he will break its back. At the end of a day's march, one elephant goes to the nearest jungle, and assists the mahout in cutting down branches for the food of the others; when these lie in a heap on the ground, he lifts up one foot, and so disposes his trunk as to make a stair for his keeper, who gets on his back with a long cord; now the beast passes up the branches one by one to him, and assists in stacking them on his own back, where they are secured by the mahout. Elephants delight in water, and will stand for hours squirting it over their own, or each other's backs, and washing their thick dark skin, and its few coarse black hairs. They have no front teeth in the lower jaw, but the under lip protudes, so as to form a sort of spout, into which they pour water from their trunks when drinking; the end of the proboscis is exceedingly sensitive, and affords to this huge beast the power of great delicacy of manipulation. On a more intimate acquaintance, he is found to be by no means as awkward or ugly an animal as might be expected; his large flabby ears are very correct, and can not only distinguish the various inflections of the human voice, but also distant sounds which are to us inaudible: his black eyes, though very small, sparkle with unmistakeable intelligence. Many elephants have no tusks, from some they have been cut off for sale, and the stumps are tipped with brass to prevent their splitting: in combat with each other, they generally lock their tusks and push head to head. The motion of riding an elephant is not unpleasant; their pace is a shambling trot, with which they get over a good deal of ground, but soon become footsore if worked too hard. Perhaps, if there is one way in which an elephant shows its intelligence more than another, it is in its dislike to gunpowder. Formerly they were much used in native warfare; but now, at the scratch of a bullet or sound of a gun, the sensible animal, having no Victoria cross to gain, or spurs to win, starts off in the opposite direction as hard as he can run, regardless of the tent on his back, or the 68-pr. in tow. As no tame elephants will breed, each has to be caught and tamed separately. The mutual dread that exists between the elephant and horse is most unaccountable, familiar with each other as a campaign must make them; they never pass without both exhibiting signs of fear, which the former sometimes gives vent to in a shrill trumpeting sound.

♂ *December* 29*th.*—Eram Cusserai. Yesterday, at noon, we arrived at this place and do not march again to-day, nor, I believe to-morrow, on account of a bridge ahead of us having been broken down. I cannot succeed in getting a comfortable saddle, and English saddles are very scarce; my pony is spirited and restless, and my saddle so uncomfortable that I have several times been nearly thrown; he never walks quietly over a little ditch, but clears it with a sudden bound that nearly unhorses me; he is very clever in scrambling over the low mud walls of this country; he has learnt the not very agreeable trick of giving the stirrup a sharp, vicious ringing kick just as one puts one foot into it when mounting, so I have to be extremely careful, or I should get my ankle broken. The aspect of the country through which we have been marching has not changed; in some places are little brooks, clumps of nice trees, fields of wheat, tobacco, or cauliflowers;

the country is nearly level with but few undulations; the trees are well grown, affording delicious shade, and generally begin to branch out at about ten feet from the ground; birds are abundant and noisy, especially green parrots; some of the houses of the natives are

TOMB AT ERAM CUSSERAI.

tastefully adorned with wood carving, and we pass others with very prettily ornamented porches, the whole of which on inspection prove to be worked in dried mud.

After the day's march, as soon as we arrive at our halting-place, we pile arms and sit down on the grass to wait for the elephants with the tents; they generally come in about twenty minutes, and when we have got our tents pitched, we go to sleep on the ground inside until the carts arrive with the baggage, which is sometimes as long as two or three hours; then we have some breakfast cooked, perform our respective toilettes, unpack a few things and spend the rest of the day in walking or

MUD PORCH AT ERAM CUSSERAI.

riding, reading or writing. We go to bed at about 8 P.M., and the next morning rise at about five, pack up our things, have a cup of coffee, and are off again before it is light. This afternoon I rode out with Captain Peel, Captain Oliver Jones, Lieut. Lind, Messrs. Garvey Watson, and Lascelles. Captain Jones is a young half-pay captain in the navy; he was formerly commander of the Hannibal in the Black Sea, and is now up here for his own pleasure. We went to see the ruins of an old town, about two miles N.N.E., called Kunnoj; this town is said to be older than Babylon, and its ruins larger than London; it was once the chief city of India, but of the old town nothing now remains but mounds of earth and bricks, which show that it must have been a place of great magnitude and importance. These mounds have in many places been tunnelled by the Hindoos, and treasure has been found in sufficient quantity to encourage people still to go on mining in peaceful times. There are many tombs and temples at Kunnoj of a comparatively modern date, although still upwards of eight hundred years old; this we ascertained by the architecture which was Hindoo, and in some places where it had been repaired, the alterations were Mussulman: the Mahommedans came into India about the year A.D. 1000.

☿ *December* 30*th.*—This afternoon I went to Kunnoj to try to make a sketch of a gateway and the tombs of two holy men: they were built of old red sandstone, which is chiefly found at Agra. To-day Brigadier Adrian Hope's brigade, consisting of the 42nd and 93rd Highlanders and 53rd arrived from Bithoor.

♃ *December* 31*st.*—6·15 A.M. Struck tents. 7·30. Proceeded on the march. P.M. 2. Halted and encamped after a march of fourteen miles. To find the

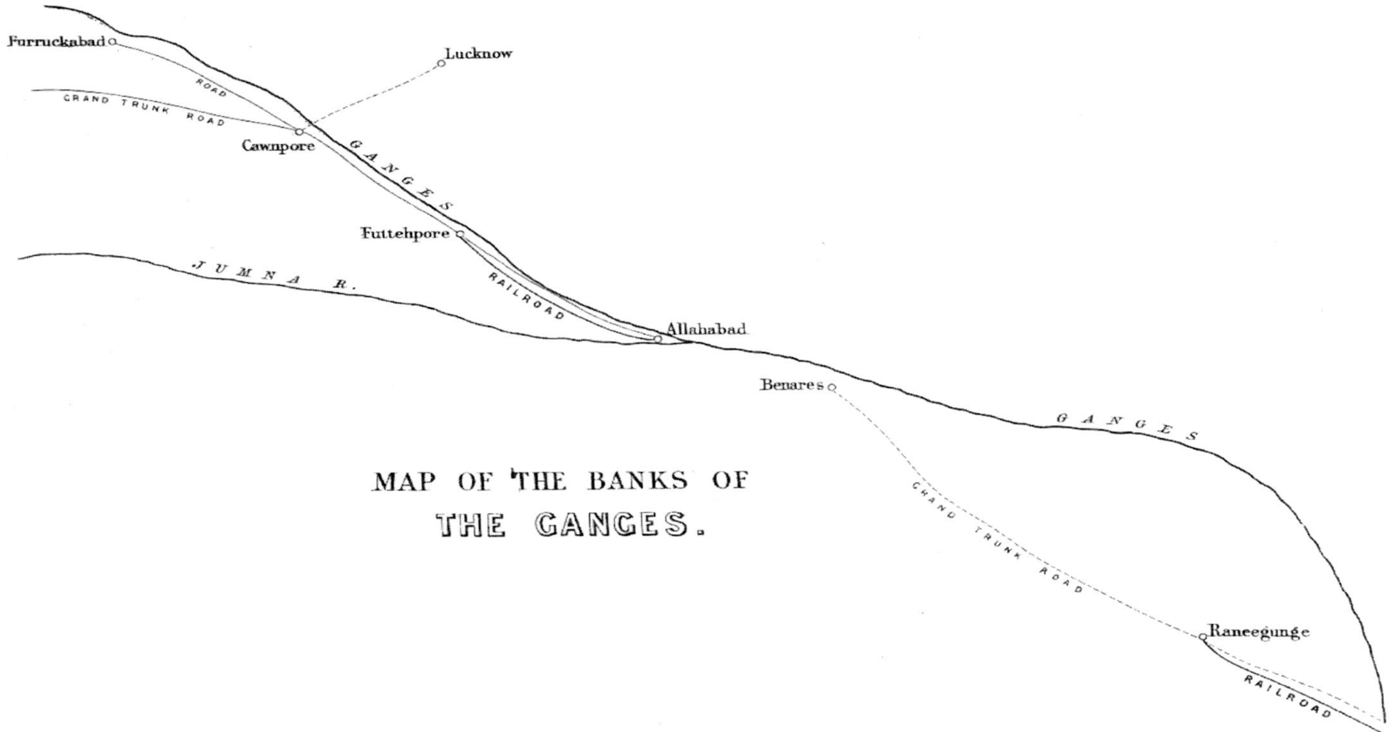

MAP OF THE BANKS OF
THE GANGES.

exact spot where we are now encamped, follow the trunk road up past Kunnoj until a by-road turns off to the right, crossing a branch of the Ganges: we are in the angle between the two roads; the enemy have broken down the bridge across the river about five miles off; the by-road leads to Futtegurh, distant about twenty-four miles. This place is called Goosai-gunge. "Gurh," as in Futtegurh, means "fort"; "Futteh" means "victory"; "gunge," as in Goosai-gunge, means "market" or "bazaar"; "pore," as in Berhampore, means "city." The ignorance that existed in England a few years ago about Indian terms, and indeed everything relating to this country is amusingly illustrated in the following story: it is said that an English M.P. read an account of a battle in the Punjaub, in which it was stated that after the engagement doolies carried off the wounded from the field. "Picture to yourselves," said the indignant gentleman, "the feelings of the sick and wounded, when just as the trumpets were sounding for victory, the ferocious doolies rushed down from the hills and carried them off." It is to be hoped that our representatives are better informed by this time. An Indian army on the line of march is a sight affording much interest and amusement; such a menagerie of men and beasts, footmen and cavalry, soldiers and sailors, camels and elephants, white men and black men, horses and oxen, Marines and Artillery, Sikhs and Highlanders.

When we first leave the encampment all is shrouded in darkness, and everyone naturally feels a little grumpy, but when the first streaks of dawn appear, and we have been an hour on the road, the welcome note is heard in the distance of the bugles sounding the "halt"; with great rapidity it passes from regiment to regiment and dies away in the rear; cavalry dismount, infantry pile arms in the middle of the road, and for a few minutes the whole army disperses on each side of it; the favourite refreshment of officers is bread, cold tongue, and "brandy-pawnee," which find their way out of innocent-looking holsters; and now we all take off overcoats or monkey-jackets which were needed when we started in the cold and damp night; the blue jackets fasten theirs over their shoulders, and the officers strap theirs to their saddles; the brief halt is too quickly at an end, and we enjoy a ten minutes' rest, when the "advance" sounds again down the line from bugler to bugler; all at once fall in, arms are unpiled, and enlivened by our band, we again step out; now feet begin to ache and boots to chafe, but the cheery music of the bands, bugles, or drums and fifes of the regiment marching next to us, generally the Rifles, infuses energy into the most footsore. We make three halts in a march of thirteen or fourteen miles, of which the last is the longest, to allow the quartermaster-general and his staff to ride on and mark out the camp. A day or two ago, an officer of a distinguished Highland regiment was observed passing the Naval Brigade on a camel; now to ride a camel at all requires some experience, but to ride one in a kilt can hardly be accounted among the pleasures of life: the individual in question, so far from appearing to enjoy himself, appeared much distressed, and in imminent danger of slipping over the camel's tail; at last his feelings became too much for him, and letting go his hold, he fell sprawling on the grass amid shouts of laughter. As the sun rises, the heat rapidly increases, and the camels and elephants are seen making short cuts across the fields, and keeping always clear of the road; when our bands have blown as much wind as they can spare into their instruments, our men strike up a song, and old windlass tunes, forecastle ditties, and many a well-known old ballad resound through the jungles or on the fertile plains of Bengal, and serve to animate our sailors and astonish the natives. The dust now becomes almost stifling, and rises in a thick cloud for eight or ten feet above the road; occasionally a staff-officer gallops by, kicking up a terrible dust; or again, a slight declivity and slope in the road shows the long and varied line of march; generally, however, it is very level, with a broad grassy glade on either side, bounded by handsome spreading trees. Our guns and ammunition follow in rear of the brigade, under the charge of a Lieutenant, with a strong guard; the small-arm ammunition is carried on camels in charge of a midshipman with a small guard. Perhaps one of the least romantic and most important offices is that of baggage-master, and every officer of the Naval Brigade will long remember the friendly care bestowed on our baggage by the Hon. Hugh Hare, an officer of the Indian army, attached to us in that capacity: owing to his exertions, it rarely happened that our baggage was not among the first to reach the new camping ground, the luxury of which will be appreciated by many an old campaigner.

♀ *January* 1*st*, 1858.—10·30 A.M. Lieuts. Wratislaw and Lind, and Mr. Garvey, mate, with two 24-prs. and one 8-in. howitzer, and double gun's crews, under command of Lieut. Vaughan, have gone to form part of a small column under Brigadier the Hon. Adrian Hope, to cover the sappers and miners while repairing a bridge over the Kallee-Nuddee, four or five miles distant. Just before Lieut. Vaughan went away, Lieut. Young and Mr. Daniel returned with the party that accompanied General Wyndham; they had blown up a large fort called Detea, shot away five or six Sepoys from guns, and hung up seventeen or eighteen of the chief men of the neighbouring villages. I have this morning bought a goat for three rupees; she will yield plenty of milk, as I shall feed her in the fields of young corn which abound; at our last camping-ground, one regiment was encamped in a potato field. I am learning to milk a goat, but cannot quite manage it yet;

I consider, myself, however, second only to Soyer in making omelettes. We get plenty of grapes, which come in caravans from Câbul, packed with cotton in little round wooden boxes; and very delicious they are too, on a dry, hot, dusty march.

♄ *January 2nd.*—At 7·30 A.M., just as the suspension bridge was repaired, the Sepoys opened fire upon our men, under Lieut. Vaughan, from a small gun in the opposite village, and our guns returned it,—the crews who were washing their garments by the river-side leaving their soap-suds and clothes, never to see them again. At eight we received orders to strike tents in half an hour; and the Naval Brigade, with their guns, the Artillery, Highlanders, Engineers, Probyn's Horse, and other regiments, were ordered to proceed immediately to the bridge. 11 A.M. Halted at the bridge. Here we found the village on the other side of the river occupied by the mutineers, with two guns. Our three guns, under Lieut. Vaughan, had crossed over the bridge, which had been repaired by the Naval Brigade during the night, and were firing from a yellow bungalow near the northern end of it, keeping up a heavy fire on the village, distant about three hundred yards; our guns now took up a position further to the left, and held in check a body of the enemy's cavalry visible beyond the village, behind the crest of some rising ground; the 53rd were lying behind the yellow bungalow, keeping up a withering fire from their skirmishers, for whom the ground afforded excellent cover from mounds and ridges of earth, and tufts of tall, coarse grass; and shortly afterwards the Lancers, and a body of Sikh cavalry, crossed the bridge and took up a position on our left; Brigadier Greathed's division then crossed over, and also formed on the left of our guns. Lieut. Vaughan now pointed and fired one of our guns at the small gun of the enemy, which was concealed behind the corner of a house, and annoying us much: his first shot struck the roof of the house; his second struck the angle of the wall about half-way down; and a third dismounted the gun and destroyed the carriage. Captain Peel, who was standing by, said, "Thank you, Mr. Vaughan; perhaps you will now be so good as to blow up the tumbril." Lieut. Vaughan fired a fourth shot, which passed near it; and a fifth, which blew it up, and killed several of the enemy. "Thank you," said Captain Peel, in his blandest and most courteous tones; "I will now go and report to Sir Colin." I was only under fire for a few minutes, when I took some ammunition over the bridge to our guns, and Captain Peel then pointed out to me the remains of the gun and tumbril. The company to which I belonged was held in reserve; but when we afterwards marched through the village, we saw the bodies of Sepoys lying near the remains of the tumbril, and fearfully burnt. After a good deal of firing, the village was stormed and captured by the 53rd, the enemy making no stand; the cavalry pursued them for some miles, capturing all their guns, eight in number, and cutting them up dreadfully. It is said that a bugler of the 53rd sounded the "advance" without orders, which excited Sir Colin's displeasure. The whole army now crossed the bridge, and proceeded about two miles to the camping-ground, distant from Futtegurh twelve miles. Casualties in the Naval Brigade, one officer and two men wounded. Captain Maxwell, of the Bengal Artillery, was brought in wounded by a musket ball through the thigh, early in the action; he was attached to the Naval Brigade as interpreter, and we shall feel the loss both of his professional services and of his agreeable society. Captain Peel met with an adventure after the capture of the village, which might have been serious; when passing through a small street, accompanied by Captain Oliver Jones, three men of the 53rd, and one or two blue jackets, five Sepoys jumped up out of a ditch on either side of the road, and rushed on them; they fought with desperation, but were all killed,—Captain Jones shooting the last man with his revolver; one man of the 53rd was dangerously wounded, but no one else on our side was hurt. Mr. Watson, an officer of the engineers, had also a narrow escape this morning: last night he was in the village, and agreed with the head man for a hundred and fifty coolies to come to assist in repairing the bridge; this morning a message came to him that they were ready, and should be delivered to any officer who came to fetch them. Watson, having some suspicions, did not go; and this saved his life, as the Sepoys were at that time in possession of the village. We reached our camping-ground at about 9·30 P.M., and parked our battery in a ploughed field, but no baggage or provisions had arrived, except the spirits, a cask of which is carried on some old limbers, and, under the charge of two quartermasters, is always foremost in the field or on the march; we were each glad to drink our day's double allowance, and even Captain Peel, who rarely drinks spirits, tossed off with gusto the abominable arrack that is served out in lieu of rum. Nearly famished, we ate every crumb in our haversacks; and I deemed myself lucky when I discovered two or three bile-wallahs making chupatties, one of which I bought for a rupee, and halved with a tent-mate. At about midnight the elephants arrived with the tents, which were immediately pitched in the total darkness; but we had not a thing else, not even a candle, till about four, when the hackeries arrived with the baggage. Every tent was then illuminated, and roaring fires blazed in rear of the camp; and at about five, as the first streaks of dawn hove in sight, we sat down to a *late* dinner.

☉ *January 3rd.*—This afternoon we marched to

Futtegurh, where we arrived at 4 P.M., and encamped on the parade-ground; the enemy abandoned the town and fort with the exception of one native officer and thirty men, with two guns, who surrendered on our arrival. The road from Kallee-Nuddee to Futtegurh, and the fields on each side of it, were strewn with dead bodies, some of old men, some of young, and some of even boys, covered with ghastly wounds; and one could trace the tracks through the fields of the flying Sepoys pursued by the relentless Sikhs, and see the trampled ground where the short, final struggle had taken place, and some of the wells we passed were choked with corpses. Near Futtegurh the road runs through groves and thickets, and among fields and orchards, separated by walls or thick banks of mud, which might have been obstinately defended.

CHAP. VI.

FURRUCKABAD AND FUTTEGURH. — PICTURE OF CAMP LIFE. — ADVANCE TO THE RAMGUNGA. — NATIVE SERVANTS. — RETURN TO CAWNPORE.

January 4th. — Futtegurh. This morning an order came out that no officer is to leave the camp without permission from the general of his division. The tents now supplied to us are square, and supported by a single pole, made of coarse canvas, and lined with blue cotton; the roofs are double, the upper one spreading out on two opposite sides into large eaves or wings. One of these is turned towards the south to keep off the sun, while the other forms the house of the native servants: on the two remaining sides are the doors, which, supported on little poles, form porches, while before the openings hang green blinds of finely-split bamboo. I have just returned from seeing a prisoner taken here, Madir Kahn; he remained in the fort till the last moment and fired a shot at us, and the Commander-in-Chief declared that if he was not given up he would burn the town down. He was at the head of the cavalry, and commanded the day before yesterday at the Kallee-Nuddee. I do not know what will be done with him, but I suppose he will either be blown away from a gun or hanged. When I saw him there was a crowd round him, some pulling his hair, and others throwing dirt in his face as he lay tied to some boards. He was a very handsome, strong-looking man, with black beard and moustaches, and richly dressed. I can hardly think it right or brave to torment a bound prisoner, however heinous his crimes may be. He lay there quite dignified and indifferent to the taunts, &c. of the crowd round him: it is said that he was a chief mover in the atrocities of Cawnpore.

♂ *January 5th.*—I went to-day to see the fort of Futtegurh, which is not to be despised. The ramparts consist of two very high and solid walls of mud with a deep ditch between; but the houses outside approach very near, and would afford excellent cover for riflemen, while there is no protection on the ramparts for the men working the guns. The fort is not very large and appeared to be nearly a square, with round mud towers at the angles, but no redans or scientific fortifications. I afterwards rode across the bridge of boats over the Ganges, and about a mile beyond the videttes into the country. It is very sandy and barren, and little tributaries cross the road, or rather track, running into the Ganges, with here and there a quicksand. When we leave Futtegurh, there are four roads open to us; the first, and I think the most probable, is that back to Cawnpore and thence to Lucknow; secondly, that leading across the country straight to Lucknow, which we are not likely to attempt with our heavy guns, as I suspect it is not a very good one; thirdly, the road to Bareilly, which I think we shall not take, as the rebels do not seem to intend to make a stand anywhere, and if we go on a wild-goose chase after them in the north, we shall leave our forces at Cawnpore and the Alumbagh unsupported. If the rebels had intended to make a stand anywhere, they would have done so at Furruckabad, which I hear is a very strong place. We hear that there are only about two thousand Sepoys gone to Bareilly, with a great mob of budmashes and rabble. Our fourth road would be that to Mynporee and Agra, where it is said that some rebels are congregated. I saw Ceely of the 42nd to-day, and he presented me with three pairs of socks, a most acceptable present, although I hear that socks are to be bought at 16*s.* a pair. Madir Kahn is to be seen hanging by the neck from a tree in the principal bazaar of Furruckabad; he said, just before he was executed, that he died with a clear conscience!

☿ *January* 6*th.*—11·30 A.M. Interred the remains of Thomas Gregory, R. M. in the station churchyard. Lieuts. Young and Wilson and Mr. Daniel, midshipman, an 8-in. howitzer and 24-pr., with a double number of oxen, proceeded with a force, under Brigadier Adrian

Hope, to Mhow, on the Bareilly road, to procure rum, of which there is a large store here, for the use of the army. Our chaplain, Mr. Bowman, is a capital shot with a gun or rifle, and sometimes brings home peacocks from the neighbouring jungle, which when roasted make no contemptible addition to a camp repast.

♀ *January* 8*th*.—P.M. Marched out for exercise; halted in an open plain, and exercised first, second, and third companies at light infantry drill. A walk through the camp in the morning is very amusing; everybody breakfasts at about nine, and hence at half-past eight all the world is dressing, &c.; in front of every tent door are one or two gallant officers enjoying their morning's bath, which ceremony is performed in this wise: the devotee, attired in the lightest conceivable dress, squats on his marrow-bones on a small board at his tent door, and his bheestie then proceeds to torture him by first letting the chilly water trickle slowly over him from the neck of his pig-skin; in vain does the victim shriek out "geldie, geldie koroo!" (quicker, quicker!) the bheestie knows his duty, and will at first only perform it in detail; gradually, however, the stream increases, and at length the very last drops are emptied in a deluge over the now shivering wretch; his bearer then presents him with towels, slippers, and brushes, and he retires from the chill morning air into his tent invigorated and refreshed as he needs be, who has the duties of a campaign to perform under an Indian sun. And passing to and fro among the tents are the charming young "dood-wallahs," every now and then repeating their musical cry "buckrie-dood," (goat's milk); these young ladies, with brass or silver bangles on their ankles, and bracelets on their wrists, contrasting with their polished black skins, and dressed in white robes with bright-coloured shawls round their heads, supply the camp with milk, and their jetty, sparkling eyes, and tall, graceful figures, surmounted by the shining brass chatty, form no unattractive addition to camp scenery. And now while their masters are breakfasting, the syce grooms and caparisons the horse of the field officer, and the bearer of the captain or subaltern gives his sword an extra rub up for the coming parade; the little cooking fires in rear of the officers quarters send up grateful odours of curries and omelettes, and little pots hiss and bubble, slyly lifting their lids, daring you to guess their contents, and shut up again with a defiant little puff of steam; and while burning green twigs crackle, subs and captains prattle, plates and dishes rattle, the bugles for parade summon all to duty; and now for a time the camp is quiet; only the native servants are left cleansing the breakfast things, the maters (sweepers) sweeping out the tents, the bheesties watering the floors, and the voices of commanding officers of different regiments break the comparative stillness; now orderly officers proceed to the head-quarters, distinguished by the union jack floating in front of the Commander-in-Chief's tent, and the camp seems deserted until regiment after regiment is dismissed, and those who are not on duty spend the heat of the day under the shadow of their tents.

☉ *January* 10*th.*—8 A.M. Mustered by companies and performed Divine service. H.M. 9th Lancers, Carabineers, Royal and Bengal Artillery attended; our chaplain, the Rev. E. L. Bowman, officiating. I have been two or three times to Furruckabad, distant three miles, and to the splendid palace which belonged to its Nawab. This is built upon a high rock, and commands a beautiful view in a northerly direction; it was intended to blow it all up, but when the mines were completed, happily the authorities changed their minds, and it is to be left standing; it is a strong fortress, and must at the same time have been a most picturesque residence, but the actual palace has been burnt. I bought from some soldiers a pair of gold-embroidered drawers, a silk table-cover, and a turban: I also took a velvet saddle from the Nawab's coach-house, where were two or three English barouches and other carriages. I found in one room a book which I brought away, and which proved to be the "Little Koran" corresponding in some degree to our prayer-book. I also inspected the Nawab's garden, where amongst other things, were two tigers in cages. The city of Furruckabad is very picturesque, and fortified in the old fashion with gates and drawbridges; it is entered through several fortified gateways from which a street or boulevard runs right through the centre of the town, with trees and walks on either side, occasionally opening out into squares. It is the handsomest Indian town I have seen, its streets are broader and its houses less squalid than those we have hitherto passed through.

☽ *January* 11*th.*—10 A.M. General parade. P.M. Exercised first and second companies at gun drill.

♂ *January* 12*th.*—A.M. Lieutenant Young and party returned from Mhow, having hung one hundred and twenty-seven rebels on one tree at that place. These dreadful though absolutely necessary severities are most painful to recollect and to commemorate. 4 P.M. Marched out for exercise, and exercised first, second, and third companies at light infantry drill.

☿ *January* 13*th.*—A party consisting of Lieutenants Hay and Wratislaw, and myself, with fifty-five men left the camp with a brigade under the command of Brigadier Walpole.

♃ *January* 14*th.*—Yesterday morning we marched away across the Ganges on the road to Shahjehanpore to the Ramgunga river, a tributary of the Ganges, on whose banks we encamped yesterday afternoon. The first part of our march was over very swampy country near the Ganges, and it was only by putting all hands on to each gun separately that we were able to proceed. We have sent our 24-pr. and 8-in. howitzer down to the banks of the Ramgunga. This river rises in the Himalayas and falls into the Ganges opposite Kunnoj; the stream here is narrow but deep, there is no ford near, and four days ago the enemy burned the bridge of boats, so that we are puzzled to know how to get over with our guns; there is talk of bringing boats overland from the Ganges, a distance of eight miles. The enemy seem to be in some force on the opposite side, with, I should think, three guns and about a hundred and fifty cavalry; they fired at us last night for about an hour, and although some of their shot pitched over our guns, no damage was done. Our brigade consists of two thousand five hundred men under command of Brigadier Walpole; Sappers, Horse Artillery, Rifle Brigade, 23rd, and detachment of Naval Brigade. Noon. About an hour ago I went down to the river with fourteen men to try to raise a sunken boat, but when the enemy saw us, they opened fire, and one shot plumped into the water about three yards from where we were all standing, which, not meeting with the approval of the engineer officer in command, he sent me and my men back again. During the night, the sappers have thrown up a pretty little breastwork in front of our guns, with the ornamental railing of a neighbouring garden forming the rear. A shot has killed three of our gun-bullocks, which we have accordingly eaten; rather an improvement on the inferior beef served out as rations.

☉ *January* 17*th.*—The day before yesterday Lieut. Vaughan brought up Lind and Garvey with two 24-prs. and their crews, so our present force here consists of six officers, one hundred and sixteen men, three guns and a howitzer. We have constructed a raft of wood and casks, under the direction of Captain Peel, who has ridden over here two or three times, and it now lies on the bank of the river all ready for launching: there is a good ford two or three miles farther down, where a boy of twelve years old could cross without being wetted above the waist: the raft is rather long and tortuous; there are besides eight boats, three of considerable size, protected by three 9-pr. guns and a very strong picquet. It is said that we are waiting here until Sir Colin receives further orders from Calcutta. We have received two elephants to draw one of our guns instead of bullocks. Yesterday we had a few drops of rain, the first intimation of the showery week that is generally met with at this time of year: the cold weather will now soon be over.

☿ *January* 20*th.*—The day before yesterday, a Sikh belonging to Hodson's Irregular Horse was severely wounded in the leg, since amputated, by a round shot, when on parade; in consequence of this, we shifted camp further back yesterday afternoon.

We are now just waiting for orders from the Commander-in-Chief, and are able to cross at any moment. We frequently receive visits from our messmates in camp at Futtegurh, but *we* are not supposed to go outside our own picquets.

♀ *January 22nd.*—Yesterday afternoon I rode down to the ford, and saw the eight boats which we have there; the river winds a good deal, so that to go to the ford by water would be a journey of perhaps five or six miles, while on this side it is only three. The country seems well cultivated, and in several places we saw topes of fine trees, but it was rather marshy. Two bodies of irregular Sikh cavalry are attached to the main army; one is distinguished by wearing red turbans, is commanded by Captain Hodson of the Indian Army, and is known as Hodson's Horse; the other wears blue turbans, is commanded by Lieut. Probyn of the Indian Army, and is known as Probyn's Horse; their dress consists of the whitey-brown "kharki;" each man is armed with a tulwa and brace of pistols, and one or two troops with lances. To command a regiment of these semi-barbarous troopers requires no small ability, tact, and personal courage, as well as knowledge of the native character, and both Probyn and Hodson are beloved by their wild horsemen. They are generally splendidly mounted, and each horse is the private property of his rider.

☽ *January 25th.*—Yesterday fell the first of the

rain that generally comes at this time of year: today is cloudy, and this morning the rain fell heavily. Yesterday afternoon I rode over to the camp at Futtegurh, slept there, and returned this morning.

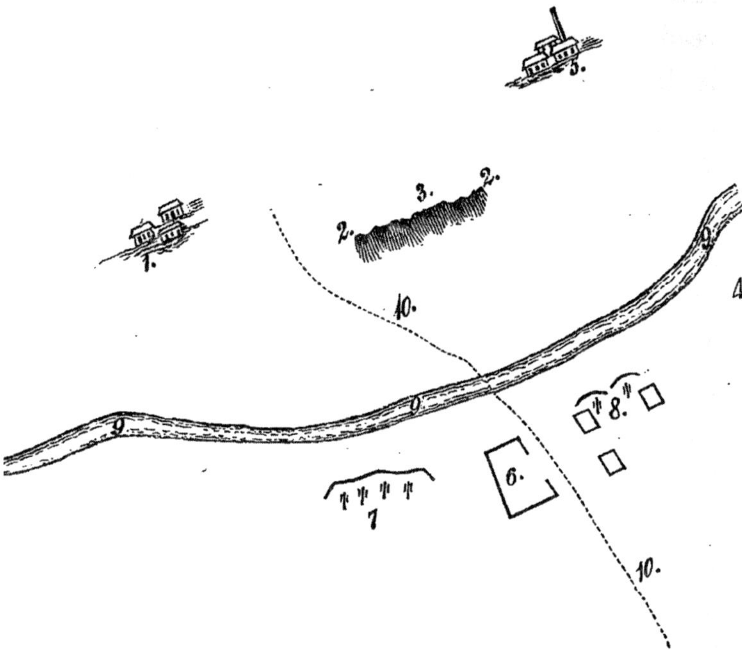

THE RAMGUNGA.

1. A village whence the enemy fire.
2. 2. Are rifle-pits.
3. A field of sugar-cane.
4. Our rifle-pits.
5. A village where the enemy have guns, one of which is a 9-pr.
6. Guard-rooms.
7. Naval Brigade Battery.
8. Horse Artillery Battery.
9. The Ramgunga river.
10. The road to Shajehanpore.

Everything was much the same as usual, only the camp had been shifted since we left. I had a nice ride there, but my poor horse had to stand in the rain all night, and it poured all the way back this morning. I took a rug with me for the horse, and at night had a couple of door mats put over him; the poor fellow has had a bad cold, and his wetting has made it no better. We are much in want of books to read, we can carry only a very few, as our baggage is limited to one camel's load. It is said that the enemy have got another heavy brass gun, which I suspect must be an 18- or 24-pr. We have roofed over a couple of mud houses near our battery for guard rooms, one for the officers and one for the blue jackets, and the former has been fitted with a table against the wall, a bed-place, and a round mud fire-place, with a hole in the roof to do duty as chimney. Yesterday a shot grazed along the roof of the guard-rooms, but did no damage beyond enlarging the chimney, and covering me with dust. The accompanying rough plan will give you some idea of our position. The enemy generally fire at our reliefs as they are marched down, but have never hit them. Yesterday a large quantity of planks and beams came from Futtegurh, and I believe that it is in contemplation to build a bridge lower down the river, where the boats are. For the future our baggage is to be carried on camels instead of in hackeries (waggons). The following is my household, a staff of six servants; first, one of our bandsmen, who is of course able to do but little for me, having to look after himself; second, my kitmagar, cook, and valet-de-chambre by name Sularoo, who receives a salary of ten rupees a month; third, my syce who looks after the ponies, brings my meals down to me in battery, cleans my shoes, and receives a salary of seven rupees a month, by name Ramjean; fourthly is my bheestie, who pours a skin full of water over me every morning, provides water for cooking, drinking, and for the horses, goat, and dog, at a salary of five rupees a month, by name Rosun: fifthly and sixthly are my two grass-cutters, who look after the ponies under the superintendance of the syce: the one of most exalted rank, who attends on the black horse is known as Mongou, and the junior one who looks after the little white baggage pony is called Beychou; they each receive a salary of five rupees a month. A rupee is of nearly the same value as a florin, and is a most convenient coin for calculations, being one tenth of a pound.

♃ *January* 28*th.*—Yesterday evening I was to have dined with Captain Fremantle of the Rifles, in his tent, but a couple of hours before dinner time he was ordered on picquet on the Futtegurh road: I begged that the invitation might be allowed to hold good to dine with him on picquet, which he kindly agreed to: accordingly at about seven in the evening, I started on my pony through the rear of the camp. Few things are more puzzling than the geography of a camp, especially by night: fires and lights are abundant, but circles of camels, rows of elephants, and streets of tents are very much alike; by dint of repeatedly asking my way, I at last came in sight of the little grove where the picquet lay; I was challenged by the sentry and led to the fire by which my friend was sitting; here a few branches had been cut down, and disposed so as to form a roof to keep off the dew, and the floor of this improvised hut was swept and strewn with hay: on this was placed a knapsack covered with a white napkin; we each brought our own knife and fork, our own servants were in attendance, and by the light of the picquet fires and a small dark lantern, the arms of the sentries glancing among the trees, the remainder of the guard sitting round their watch fire with song and jest, I enjoyed as good a dinner as ever I had in my life.

♂ *February 2nd.*—Yesterday at 3 A.M. we struck tents, and at 4 marched for our old camping ground at Futtegurh, where we now are; and so I suppose that the Sepoys will boast that they have driven us off. At the same time that we left Ramgunga, the main body of the army marched from this place, and were to proceed to Cawnpore.

☿ *February 3rd.*—Futtegurh. My little horse has at last recovered from the very serious cough that has laid him up for the last fortnight: I sometimes rig up a hurdle on the parade ground for him to jump over, which he does admirably. The Sepoys have crossed the Ramgunga river on whose bank we were encamped, and are now not far from the N. E. bank of the Ganges: perhaps our late retrograde movement has increased their confidence, as well as the fact that the floating bridge has been taken to pieces for the purpose of moving it lower down the river. The habits that Europeans acquire in this country are certainly most luxurious: for instance, even when campaigning, unless we are actually under weigh, the first thing that awakens me in the morning is my kitmagar with a cup of delicious coffee: I drink this, half awake, and go to sleep again on the other side, and presently have visions of a warm water lather on my face, and the light touch of a keen razor, wielded by a skilful and unerring hand; a soft handkerchief dipped in warm water seems to be gently passed over my chin, and when I wake about an hour afterwards, lo! I am shaved.

♃ *February 4th.*—This morning we left Futtegurh and marched twelve miles. I saw this afternoon an enraged elephant, commonly called a "bobbery-wallah." He walked straight through the two sides of an uninhabited house, and then with his tusks and trunk began unroofing and pulling down the next one, throwing the pieces of mud and wood in all directions; the owner of the house sat on a neighbouring wall wringing his hands, and uttering the most piteous lamentations: the mahout sat quietly on the animal's neck kicking its head to make it go away; after some time this discipline took effect, the animal became more quiet, and returned by the way that it came.

February 5th.—This morning we passed the suspension bridge over the Kallee-Nuddee, where we licked the Sepoys on the 2nd of January. Between this place and Futtegurh, the sides of the roads were ornamented with the skeletons of Sepoys, whose grinning skulls were as clean as a knife-handle, having been skilfully picked by the jackalls. From being constantly led on the march, and having always to make his home where I make mine, my horse has learnt to follow me like a dog; and this tameness shows itself in most other horses; they do not wish to run away, because they have nowhere to run to. We hear of reports circulated of the barbarities practised by the Sepoys upon our countrymen and women, which we believe to be greatly exaggerated; this is a war in which the worst passions are likely to be excited, and without doubt dreadful scenes have been enacted; but I have heard of great cruelties being perpetrated by our own people during some of the sieges in Spain and elsewhere, yet we claim to be the most enlightened nation in the world, and the Sepoys are comparatively savages. It seems to be a general opinion that in this case a war of extermination *must* be carried on, at any rate for the present, but I feel the greatest compassion for our enemy. It is idle to speak of the benefits we have heaped upon them; they regard every Christian as lower than a dog, and therefore every benefit is an additional insult; if a European makes use of a native drinking-pot, no Hindoo will drink out of it again, but will throw it away, unless it be of brass, and then he will kindle a fire in it to purify it. The Hindoo is not by nature such an abject being, but circumstances have made him simulate it up to the present time, and I regard them with pity and almost admiration, though this is a sentiment that I cannot expect to be shared by those whose dearest friends have been their victims.

☽ *February 8th.*—Castor-oil bushes abound on this road; the nut is by no means of a disagreeable taste, but rather the reverse, and is, I believe, as efficacious a medicine as the oil; I wish the doctors would give us the nut instead of its most nauseous extract. We halted this afternoon about thirty-one miles from Cawnpore, and hope to arrive there the day after to-morrow. We hear that the Sepoys we left at Ram-gunga have all gone to Lucknow.

♂ *February 9th.*—To-day we passed the ground where we were encamped on Christmas Day. Nothing can be more desolate than the appearance of a deserted camping-ground; it is astonishing to see the harm that ten thousand men and their followers can do in one night; in an old camping-ground one can trace the lines of the several camps, the places where the horses were picqueted, and where the elephants slept; the ground is strewn with worn-out shakos and accoutrements, broken pots and kettles, old boots and rags, the ashes of camp-fires, and other *débris;* altogether, I think it is one of the most doleful sights in the world, calling up, as it often does, a few happy hours spent there when it was teeming with life, the camp-fires burning brilliantly, and the merry laugh and jest passing from tent to tent; perhaps an hour or two afterwards the spot is peopled with loathsome, howling jackalls, who have been prowling about waiting to pick up any or all offal that may be left behind. Shortly after our camp was pitched, a hare started up and ran through it, and eventually escaped, though chased by various men and dogs; about half an hour afterwards, a small deer started up, and, after being nearly caught, also succeeded in making its escape.

☿ *February* 10*th.*—I rode into Cawnpore this evening in advance of Brigadier Walpole's brigade, to announce their vicinity. I dined with Captain Peel, who showed me a wonderful hen; every evening she comes into his tent, and cackles until he places his portmanteau across one corner, when she retires behind it for the night, and the next morning lays an egg.

♃ *February* 11*th.*—This morning the whole of Brigadier Walpole's brigade—*i. e.* the 2nd and 3rd battalions of the Rifle Brigade, H.M. 23rd, and detachment of the Naval Brigade with four guns, under command of Lieut. Vaughan—rejoined the main army, which to-morrow morning starts for Lucknow, towards which place Mr. Church, with two guns, under the command of Lieut. Wilson, have gone with an advanced brigade this evening; we are now encamped on the south side of Cawnpore.

CHAP. VII.

MARCH TO UNAO. — NAVAL BRIGADE RACES. — BUNTERA. — BREAKING UP THE ENCAMPMENT AT NIGHT. — LUCKNOW. — CAPTURE OF THE DILKUSHAH.

♀ *February* 12*th.*—4·30 A.M. Struck tents and proceeded across the bridge of boats over the Ganges towards Lucknow. These bridges of boats over the Indian rivers are very remarkable, and it is only by this plan that they can be bridged, except at a very great expense; they have to be reconstructed every year. As soon as the floods, brought on by the rains, begin to fall, a number of large boats, of some fifteen or twenty tons, are securely moored across the river, with the exception of two in the middle, which can be removed to allow trading craft to pass; planks are laid across from one end to the other, and covered with straw and earth; large platforms are then laid down on the soft mud from the bridge to the firm ground. When the river begins to swell in autumn, the platforms are floated away and secured for the succeeding year, and all the barges are moored together. After marching twelve miles, we encamped at Unao. H.M. 53rd accompanied us, also our siege-train, consisting of six 24-prs., six 8-inch 56-prs., two 8-inch howitzers, and eight rocket tubes.

♄ *February* 13*th.*—Unao. The right wing of H.M. 93rd Highlanders arrived in camp. Yesterday morning, on our arrival here, all the men of the 53rd left their tents, came out to meet us, and gave us a cheer; when the 93rd arrived this morning, our men with one consent ran out to meet them, and as they approached gave them three cheers; when they passed our guns, where Captain Peel was standing with his officers, they carried arms, and our band played "Auld lang syne."

☽ *February* 15*th.*—Unao. To-day the Naval Brigade races took place, and Captain Peel was umpire; I rode my pony in a steeple-chase, but when going over the course for the fifth and last time, with both stirrup-leathers broken, in taking the last hurdle, neck and neck with the leading horse, my pony fell, and we rolled over and over in the dust together: I was stunned but not hurt, but my pony sprained his shoulder rather severely. Much amusement was created by two of our blue jackets racing on water-buffaloes, urged on by half a dozen men before and behind.

☿ *February* 17*th.*—Unao. Every evening we have battery drill, and run our very heavy battery about near the camp; sometimes we form square to receive cavalry, with guns on three faces and the limbers in the rear, and at other times we change the front of the battery with great rapidity, as in light infantry drill. The Commander-in-Chief witnessed our parade this evening, and expressed his approbation of the way in which our men worked the guns. With drag-ropes, and eighteen or twenty men to each gun, we run them about very well, and really Captain Peel has a splendid command. On the march our guns are each drawn by twenty-two bullocks, or two elephants; if a gun sticks in the mud, it becomes a most serious matter, as it is no easy task to persuade eleven pairs of bullocks to pull together; but by taking them out, manning the wheels and drag-ropes with blue jackets, and having an elephant to push behind with his forehead, we never fail to extricate a gun from the worst swamps.

☉ *February* 21*st.*—Unao. The third battalion of the Rifle Brigade arrived from Cawnpore. Performed divine service; present the Naval Brigade, Royal Artillery, and 42nd Highlanders.

☾ *February* 22*nd.*—Unao. We are still waiting for orders to proceed to Lucknow; the usual routine of the day is a ride before parade; at 9 A.M. parade with drill, then breakfast, and sedentary employments throughout the day; at four in the afternoon, parade followed by battery drill, and this succeeded by dinner finishes up the day. Lieut. Vaughan has been promoted to the rank of commander.

♃ *February* 25*th.*—4·30 A.M. Struck tents and proceeded on the march, twelve miles, to Buntera: at Bunny Bridge, Lieut. Wilson, with his detachment, joined us, and proceeded with the 79th Highlanders and ourselves to the camping ground. The march of an army at four o'clock in the morning is a very picturesque sight. At about three you are awakened by your servant bringing in a cup of hot coffee and a chupattie, a sort of cake, and then you perceive that everything in the tent has been packed up, except the clothes about to be put on: the carpets lie rolled up in a corner; the tables and their folding legs are tied together, ready to be placed on the elephant that carries the tent; all the tent pegs have been knocked out except four which just keep the pole from falling; and as we wish each other good morning and sip our coffee, the boatswain's mates pipe "down tents;" we hurry on our things, but before we are dressed our charpoys (light bedsteads) are carried out, and the bedding rolled up, and as the last of us steps out of the door, the calassies (tent-men) drive out the remaining pegs, and down falls the tent: now all appears to be chaos: large fires are burning, consuming the refuse of the encampment; their fitful lurid glare distorts all shadows, and only seems to make darkness visible; the cries of the natives, the moanings and gurglings of camels, the trumpetings of elephants, the buglings of neighbouring regiments, and the shrill pipe of our boatswain's mate add to the confusion: and occasionally a frightened bobbery elephant rushes past in the darkness, regardless of the sharp iron point which the mahout is driving into the back of his neck; presently a few lances glimmer in the fire-light; we hear the jingling of accoutrements, and the Commander-in-Chief rides swiftly by, attended by his staff and a small cavalry escort. At last the boatswain's mates pipe all together — a pause — and we hear "Hands fall in:" immediately everything must be left, baggage, tents, or breakfasts, and we all find our respective companies in the darkness. Captain Vaughan's clear voice rings out: "*Naval Brigade, attention!*" "*Fours right,*" "*By your left, quick march!*" and away we go, our band playing the Rifle Brigade March "I'm ninety-five." News have arrived that Brigadier Grant, with a force, went out from Buntera and attacked the rebels at a place about twelve miles off, called Meangunge, taking four guns, and killing four hundred and fifty Sepoys. The Queen's Bays have to-day joined the army; as they passed our tents, one horse reared, and rising perpendicularly on his hind legs, overbalanced himself and fell back on his rider; to my astonishment both got up and shook themselves, the trooper remounted and took up his place again in the troop. The breech-loading carbine, with which this regiment is armed, is very heavy even if held with both hands but yet is intended to be fired with one hand only.

February 26th.—Buntera. The great question in England now seems to be "How are we to govern India?" Ought it not rather to be "What sort of people are now thrown upon our hands to be governed?" There seems to be some idea that, since we have shown our military superiority, we can govern India as we like; but this is far from being the case; the rebellion, except in Oude, has been confined entirely to the one class, the Sepoys; over them only have we shown our superiority, and not over the mass of the Hindoos. I do not believe that the mutiny has been caused, by the Civil Government, though that may also have been defective, but by military misrule, and the contempt for the natives so universal among the English in the country. If any indiscreet measures are introduced by the new form of government, whatever that may be, I should not be surprised if they were followed by a revolt more serious than the present mutiny. Some few Hindoos have commanded my respect and sympathy, for all I feel much pity. They contain the elements of a fine and noble people, and it remains to be seen whether religion and civilisation will precipitate the dross, or whether harsh measures are indispensable. The accounts we hear of the fertility of India, its aptness for railroads, the abundance of water for agricultural purposes, and its various climates suitable for the production of every tree, vegetable, or flower in the world, are in no degree exaggerated. The governing of such an invaluable country as India might become, is a subject which cannot receive too much consideration, and so inexhaustible that a life-time would not be thrown away upon it. I think that much harm is done in this country by Englishmen who have made a good deal of money out here, and encourage a feeling of contempt for the natives. It is indeed a great puzzle how India is to be governed; at present, the English in the country are *all* gentlemen; there is no class that is considered as the aristocracy, except a few officials at Calcutta; there is no lower class, except a very few English servants; the country is therefore ruled by the magistrates and a few of the richer natives, while all the labouring work is done by the Hindoos: from all which I gather that the simplest way to rule India would be to colonise it; to *make* a lower class who would farm and cultivate the land themselves, which in many parts might be done, except perhaps during the three hottest months. I can see too that the English in the country despise the Hindoos, especially since the mutiny, quite as much as the Hindoos despise them: one great difficulty with which the government has to grapple is the attachment to caste.

☉ *February* 28*th.* — To-day the sacrament was administered by the Rev. Mr. Ross, in the mess-tent of the 42nd Highlanders, and amongst others present was Brigadier Adrian Hope. This holy rite, performed in a foreign land, amid the bustle and hurry of a camp, on the bare earth, with a few yards of canvas for a covering, was most impressive, and conveyed a lesson of the omnipresence of the Almighty, which will long be remembered by the few who knelt together on that day. This morning, Sir Colin Campbell left Cawnpore, and passed us on his way to Alumbagh, returning here in the evening, a ride of upwards of sixty miles. The activity of our veteran chief, tires out many younger members of his Staff.

March 2nd.—Yesterday I went to see the Alumbagh, and paid a visit to my friend Major Guise of the 90th. The Alumbagh was formerly the residence of the queen-mother. For a palace the house is rather small; it is at present surmounted by a telegraph and surrounded by a walled garden: the latter has been almost completely destroyed, and is cut up in all directions by zig-zags leading to batteries at its angles. There is also a battery in front of the main gate. The Alumbagh is about three miles from Lucknow, and from the top of the house the beautiful domes and minarets of the city are plainly visible. No firing, except from small arms, was going on during my visit. The palace must formerly have been beautifully ornamented, as the walls are still prettily painted. Afterwards we rode to Jellalabad, which is about one mile distant from the Alumbagh; it is a curious old fort, with very strong thick mud walls, which we are now putting into a tolerable state of defence, to be used as a large depository for all sorts of commissariat stores. On my return to camp, the news arrived of Captain Peel's appointment as A.D.C. to Her Majesty, and receiving the decoration of K.C.B. Yesterday morning, there was an alarm that the Sepoys were attacking us, and the whole army got under arms; but it turned out to be all a mistake. Captain Peel went away this morning at four o'clock, with two guns and two howitzers, under command of Lieut. Young, and I believe that he is gone with Sir Colin and other troops to occupy the Dilkushah, which will probably give them a little fighting.

☿ *March 3rd.* — Last night, at half-past ten, just as we had all comfortably turned into bed and were enjoying our first doze, orders arrived to strike tents and proceed on the march; so there was no help for it but to turn out again. We marched the whole night in company with the 93rd and 42nd Highlanders, and did not reach our camping-ground, in rear of the Dilkushah, until 10·30 A.M. Our march was only seven miles, but it lasted twelve hours, on account of the narrowness and bad state of the roads, losing our way in the dark, and the difficulty we experienced in getting our guns through the tortuous approaches of the ancient fortress of Jellalabad. The Dilkushah was taken yesterday afternoon, with but little loss; we had two men mortally wounded. I went there to-day; it is a fine-looking old house, commanding a splendid view from the upper balconies. On the right is the blue winding river Goomtee, an inconsiderable stream at this time of year, with fertile plains stretching beyond it. On the right front is that splendid building the Martinière College, having two guns at one corner doing a good deal of mischief to our battery of four guns. In front of the Martinière is a loop-holed wall, used by the Sepoys as a rifle-pit, and opposed by a similiar one for our riflemen. In front of the Dilkushah is another gun, partially concealed by trees; in the distance are seen the domes and minarets of Lucknow, looking not unlike a view of Stamboul from the land side: on the left stands our camp. I remained in our battery for about an hour, the firing not being very heavy, or the enemy's guns particularly well aimed.

CHAP. VIII.

SIEGE OF LUCKNOW.—SIR JAMES OUTRAM CROSSES THE GOOMTEE. —CAPTURES OF THE MARTINIÈRE, BEGUM KOTHEE, LITTLE IMAUM-BARAH, AND KAISER-BAGH.

♃ *March 4th.*—To-day our guns all came into park, being replaced by four artillery guns, which took up the position. We have buried one of our petty officers, named Terry, who had been doing duty as sergeant-major; he was severely wounded by a round shot in the upper part of the leg; the same shot wounded another man, who still survives, carrying away a portion of his skull and brain. Captain Oliver Jones, who is serving as a volunteer with H. M. 53rd, has distinguished himself, being the second to mount a breach at the capture of a neighbouring fort; he received a wound on the knuckles, but cut down the fellow who gave it to him. A bee has made herself a nest in a hole in our bamboo tent-pole, and there she lives as snug as possible; in the day time she comes out and flies about, at night creeps into her nest, and on the march travels in her tent-pole; I am not sure that we have not got a pair; we frequently see one passing in or out, the hole being of about this

size and shape. I hear that we have with us pontoons, and when at Jellalabad the other day I saw a portable raft on empty casks floating on a pond with a gun on it.

♀ *March* 5*th.*—Here is a rough plan to give some idea of our battery. *a*, is the river Goomtee; *b*, is the

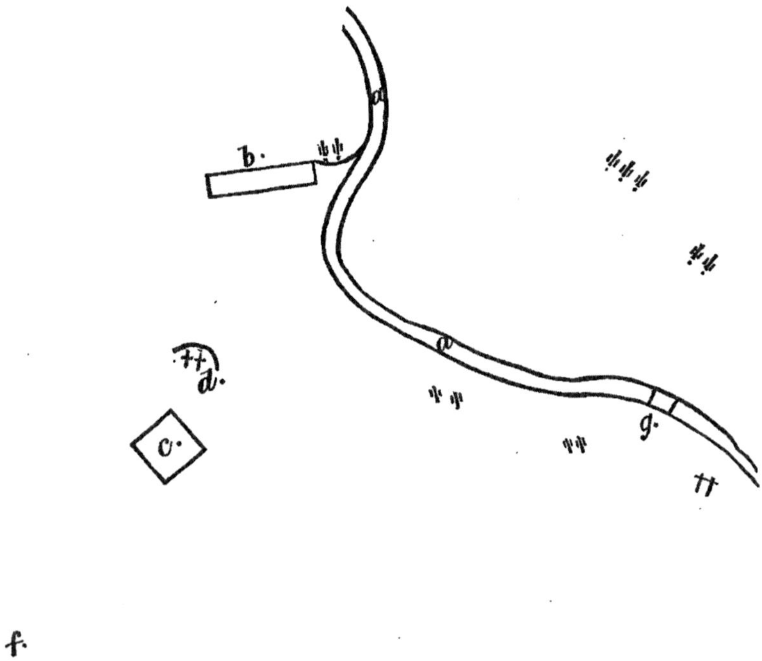

PLAN OF THE SHANNON'S NAVAL BRIGADE BATTERY.

Martinière; *c*, the Dilkushah; *d*, is the battery I visited the day before yesterday, which was then held by our guns, but is now in charge of the siege-train. *e*, is the position of Lucknow; *f*, of our camp; *g*, represents two bridges across the Goomtee, only one of which is as yet finished. The artillery guns are marked † † those of the Naval Brigade , and the enemy's guns, as near as I could guess, . We left camp this morning at half-past nine, with two guns and four guns crews under the command of Lieut. Wilson, with Lieut. Wratislaw and Mr. Richards, who passed for a midshipman about a fortnight ago: we had not brought our guns into position ten minutes, before the Sepoys opened fire on us from their two guns at the corner of the Martinière, and the second or third shot struck the ground within six feet of where I stood and enveloped me in a cloud of dust; my comrades thought I was killed, and were surprised to see me standing in the same place when the dust cleared away. I should not wonder if an attack were made on the bridge to-night; it is constructed of wood lashed on empty casks, and appears to be well and strongly put together: the enemy are keeping up an occasional fire of round shot on it, but are doing no damage, as it is protected by the banks of the Goomtee. At 8 P.M. the enemy opened fire with shells made of brass, which we did not return, and they were then quiet for the remainder of the night.

♄ *March* 6*th*.—Here is another rough outline of our position: *a*, is the Dilkushah; *b*, the Martinière; *c*, is Lucknow; and *d*, the Goomtee; *e*, shows the position of the two bridges, and *f*, of the guns which annoyed us yesterday; this morning at 2 A.M. thirty guns of Horse Artillery, H.M. 23rd Fusileers, and 79th Highlanders, the 1st Bengal Fusileers, and Cavalry, under command of Sir James Outram, began crossing

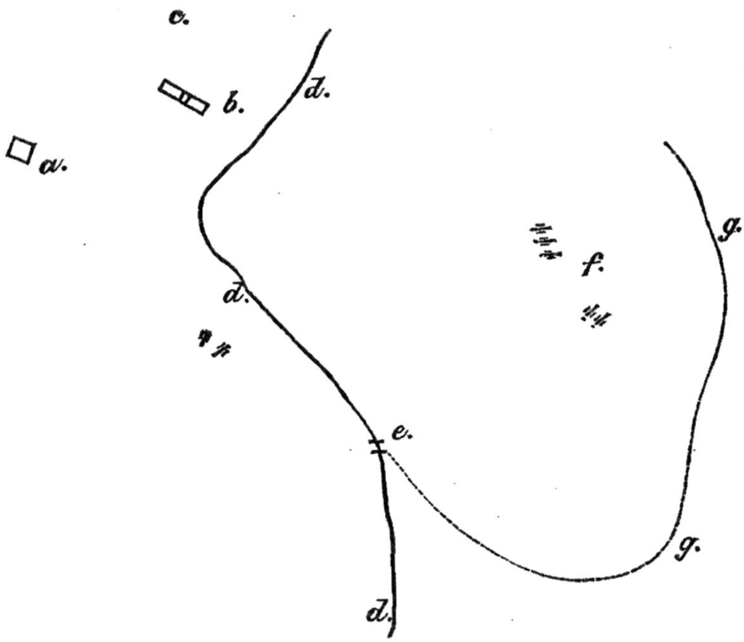

OUTLINE OF THE SHANNON'S NAVAL BRIGADE POSITION.

the river, and, proceeding by the track I have marked *g*, took in rear the guns marked *f*, and are now marching towards where the old cantonments stood. While the troops were crossing, I observed a young man in spectacles on a small pony, riding unobtrusively about, giving a quiet order here and stopping a dispute there, always listened to with respect; I inquired who he was, and learned that it was General Mansfield, the Chief of the Staff. At daylight the enemy opened fire upon the troops crossing, which we returned, and then changed the position of our guns further to the left. At 10 A.M. we observed the Horse Artillery and Cavalry engaging the enemy among the topes of trees on the other side of the river from which they were effectually driven and their guns captured. Sir James Outram has siege guns with him, so Lucknow will be threatened from three points—the Alumbagh, the Dilkushah, and the cantonments where Sir James is in force. We slept very comfortably in battery last night, except when a little rain fell.

☉ *March 7th.*—This day has been comparatively quiet, an occasional fire only being kept up on the Martinière.

☾ *March 8th.*—This afternoon we withdrew our guns from the river, so now all our battery is together in park.

♂ *March 9th.*—At 3 A.M. our six 8-in. guns and two 24-prs. went down in front of the Dilkushah, with four rocket hackeries, the whole under command of Captain Vaughan, accompanied by Lieuts. Young, Salmon, and Wratislaw, Mr. Daniel, and Lords Walter Kerr and Arthur Clinton, midshipmen; Captain Peel is also down there with his two A.D.C.'s Watson and Lascelles. In giving the strength of the Naval Brigade, I have heretofore forgotten to mention two brass field-pieces, a 6-pr. and a 24-pr. howitzer, also eight rocket tubes mounted on hackeries. When General Grant was away with his brigade, and took the fort of Meangunge, about seven hundred mutineers were executed, and to save ammunition five were placed one behind the other; it was then found that a Minié bullet passed through the bodies of the first four and killed the fifth. Yesterday I rode over the Goorkahs' camp, but did not find them such short men as I had been led to expect. With their celebrated knives, they are said to cut off a bullock's head with one blow. Even now, as I am writing, Watson, Captain Peel's A.D.C. arrives with the news that he has been wounded; he went out with his usual nonchalance to find a suitable place for some guns to be posted to breach the outer wall of the Martinière, when he was shot in the thigh by a musket ball; he was taken to the Dilkushah, and the bullet extracted by the surgeon of the 93rd Highlanders. The wound is dangerous, it having been necessary to cut the ball out from the opposite side of the leg to that at which it entered: this news causes us all the deepest concern, as we have such great admiration and regard for him. At 2 P.M. several regiments marched to the Dilkushah to be ready to storm the Martinière: at 3, the 42nd and 93rd Highlanders with some artillery and Sikhs left the Dilkushah and got under cover of a wall two or three hundred yards from the Martinière; a heavy fire of musketry was kept up by the enemy as the troops marched down, but no casualties occurred: after a short time the Highlanders rushed into the open and crossed the field to the Martinière, hardly a shot being fired: as soon as the enemy saw us preparing to storm they withdrew their guns, evacuated their trenches, and fled to the rear of the Martinière, leaving that building in our possession without the loss of a man. As soon as we had occupied it, a heavy fire was opened upon us from the first line of defences in its rear, but this, being enfiladed by Sir James Outram from the opposite side of the river was stormed and captured by the Highlanders on the same evening.

☿ *March* 10*th*.—This morning one of our men was slightly wounded in the lower part of the leg; this is our first casualty, with the exception of Captain Peel's wound of yesterday, and the two men mortally wounded at the capture of the Dilkushah. We know very little of what goes on in the front, as we are obliged to remain in camp in case we are wanted, and we cannot believe all the reports that reach us. To-morrow I am ordered down to relieve the battery with Richards, midshipman, and the whole of the first company under command of Lieut. Wilson: our guns have now pushed on to Banks's bungalow. I went this afternoon to see that palatial building the Martinière; it is indeed splendid in design and perfect in execution, and the view from the top is very extensive and magnificent. Captain Peel is going on as well as can be expected. Several regiments have moved to-day into the park in front of the palace of the Dilkushah, which, as well as the Martinière, will be used as a hospital. I went to the corner of the latter where the enemy had those two guns that did them such good service: a bank rising on one side afforded good natural protection, and accounts for our having been unable to dismount their guns with our shot. In front of the college is an artificial lake from the centre of which rises a single column on an arched foundation, water in this climate being an essential in a "parterre."

♃ *March* 11*th.*—Opened fire on the Begum's palace, and advanced an 8-inch howitzer on the right. 1 P.M. Advanced two guns on the right front to within about a hundred and fifty yards of the Begum Kothee. 4·30. The Begum Kothee stormed and captured by H.M. 90th and the 93rd Highlanders, and regiment of Feroozepore, supported by H.M. 38th and the 42nd Highlanders.

♀ *March* 12*th.*—Yesterday, about the middle of the day, I came down with the first company to relieve battery. We found our men at (1), where we had three guns; we had also guns at Banks's Bungalow (2); at the same time Captain Vaughan commanded another battery at about (4); while we were busily employed breaching the wall of the Begum's palace at (6) from (1),

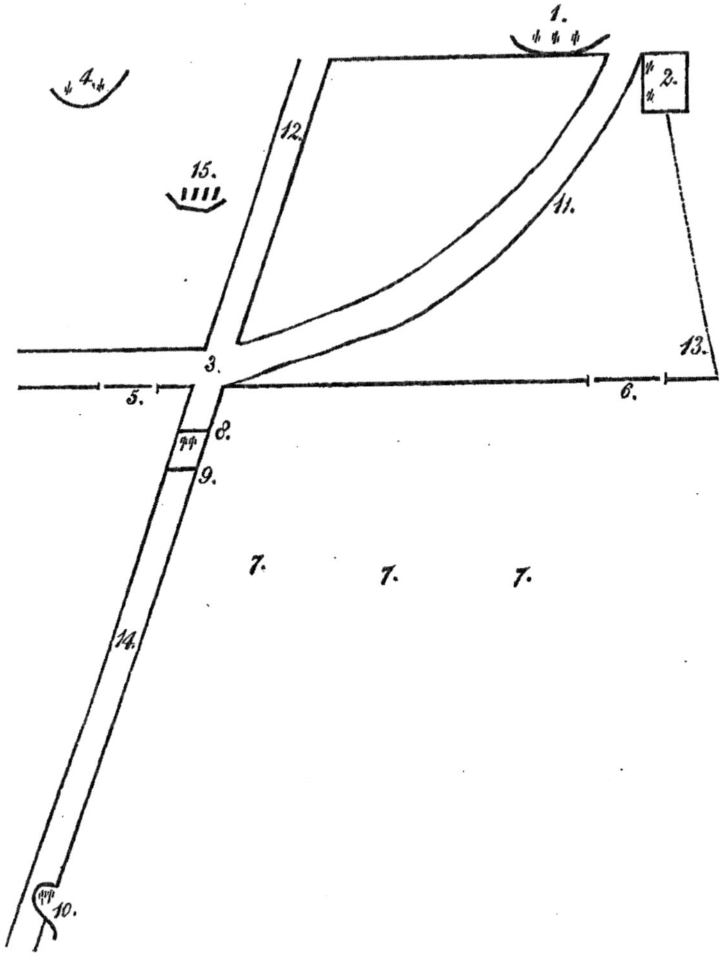

PLAN OF ATTACK ON THE BEGUM'S PALACE.

and Captain Vaughan was breaching another wall at (5) from (4), we heard the sad news that poor Garvey had just been killed by a shell from one of our own mortars at (15). He was riding very fast to deliver a message, and had occasion to pass before a row of cohorns; he did not see that the quick-matches were alight until too late to stop, and the charges igniting, one shell struck him on the head, causing of course instantaneous death; the horse on which he was riding escaped unhurt. Thus for the second time we have lost one of our most promising young officers, and I have lost an intimate friend and affectionate messmate. Poor Garvey! he had a warm heart. At about 5 P.M. the breach was considered practicable; General Sir Robert Napier decided on the precise moment when the firing should cease; officers commanding batteries, and those told off to lead the storming parties compared their watches. At this moment an officer, in a half-Oriental half-European uniform, mounted on a magnificent Arab, galloped up, followed by half-a-dozen native officers gorgeously dressed and also mounted on Arabs; it was Captain Hodson of Hodson's Horse, and this was the last time we were to behold the gallant fellow. It was a sight worth seeing that Englishman commanding and holding in check such a wild body of Sikhs, and yet beloved by them and admired by all who knew him; and even his dress was striking, the red turban on his head, and the cashmere scarf round his waist showing his connection with his wild horsemen. He dismounted, and leaving his horse in our battery, exchanged a few pleasant words with us, and walked cheerily down to where the storming party were anxiously awaiting the agreed-on moment. A few seconds before their time, the storming party of the gallant 93rd rushed from their cover, led several yards ahead by their noble commander Captain Clarke, who ran up to the breach waving his sword and shouting out "Come on, 93rd!" His men gave one loud and continuous cheer, some hoisting their bonnets on the points of their bayonets, and in a few moments the space between our battery and the breach was swarming with kilted Highlanders. Suddenly, however, came a check, as they found that a deep trench had been cut in front of the wall: this however had been foreseen by Sir Robert Napier who had ordered a house to be knocked into where he supposed it would be (13); to this point the troops now swarmed, and crossing the ditch disappeared behind the wall. From this time little more could be seen from our battery; occasionally a few Sepoys would be observed clambering over a wall or along the roof of a house, and one would make good his escape, and another would fall back shot through; and occasionally a soldier appearing on the wall, perhaps in pursuit of a fugitive, would be greeted with a sailor's cheer; the air resounded with the cries of the wounded and dying, the cheers of our soldiers, and the echoes of a dropping fire, it was at this time that Captain Hodson was mortally wounded. Gradually, as all became still, we knew that the enemy's second line of defence was captured, and the Begum Kothee was in our hands; at the same time that the 93rd stormed at (6), another party stormed opposite Captain Vaughan's battery at (5), and were equally victorious. A gun from our battery, and a gun from the battery at (4), then advanced down the road to (3), Captain Vaughan coming by the road marked (12), and we by that marked (11); thence we began firing over the Sepoys' earthwork at (8), back through their own embrasures, at a confused multitude of them retreating down the road, (14) to (10), where they had a semi-circular battery: once safe in this they opened a smart fire on us, which would have done much harm, as they knew our distance so accurately, had we not been protected by their own earthwork: we could not see over it to point our guns, but Captain Oliver Jones, at no small personal risk, planted himself on the top and directed our fire. We took the Sepoy guns at (8), and during last night moved our two guns round to a breastwork we had thrown up at (9), where they now are, and the rest of them into park in a neighbouring garden. The Sepoys in derision have hoisted the union jack over their circular battery. Last night I went into the breach that we had made, and found the courts and gardens covered with the bodies of slain Sepoys: I went there again this morning, and saw a deep ditch full of them. At the back of the palace was a small chapel, full of Korans and chandeliers, such as are to be seen in every mosque. The palace had been fitted up beautifully, the walls ornamented with splendid mirrors and the ceilings with chandeliers; everything of this kind was of course smashed, but those men who first got in found numbers of cashmere shawls, valuable silks, &c., and even a few gold mohurs. Last night we slept at our guns, which we did not find unpleasant, the weather being quite warm, but the flies and mosquitoes rather uncourteous.

♄ *March* 13*th.*—This afternoon I went down to our guns, and found that they had advanced, as in the plan: *a* is the advanced wall of the Begum's palace which was taken on the 11th; *b* is an entrance we made in it for our guns to advance to the court *c*, having a mosque in the centre; they then passed through the wall by a hole *d* into the yard *m*, and thence by a breach at *e*, through a long shed *f*, to a gate *g*, where a breastwork was thrown up for them; our troops then took possession of the houses *j* and the garden *n*, and commenced a withering fire upon the Sepoys who were in the house *i*, and all along the opposite side of the street *h*, which is about twenty yards wide; *k* is the small Imaum-barah, the immediate object of attack, to reach which it is first necessary to breach two walls. The Imaum-barah

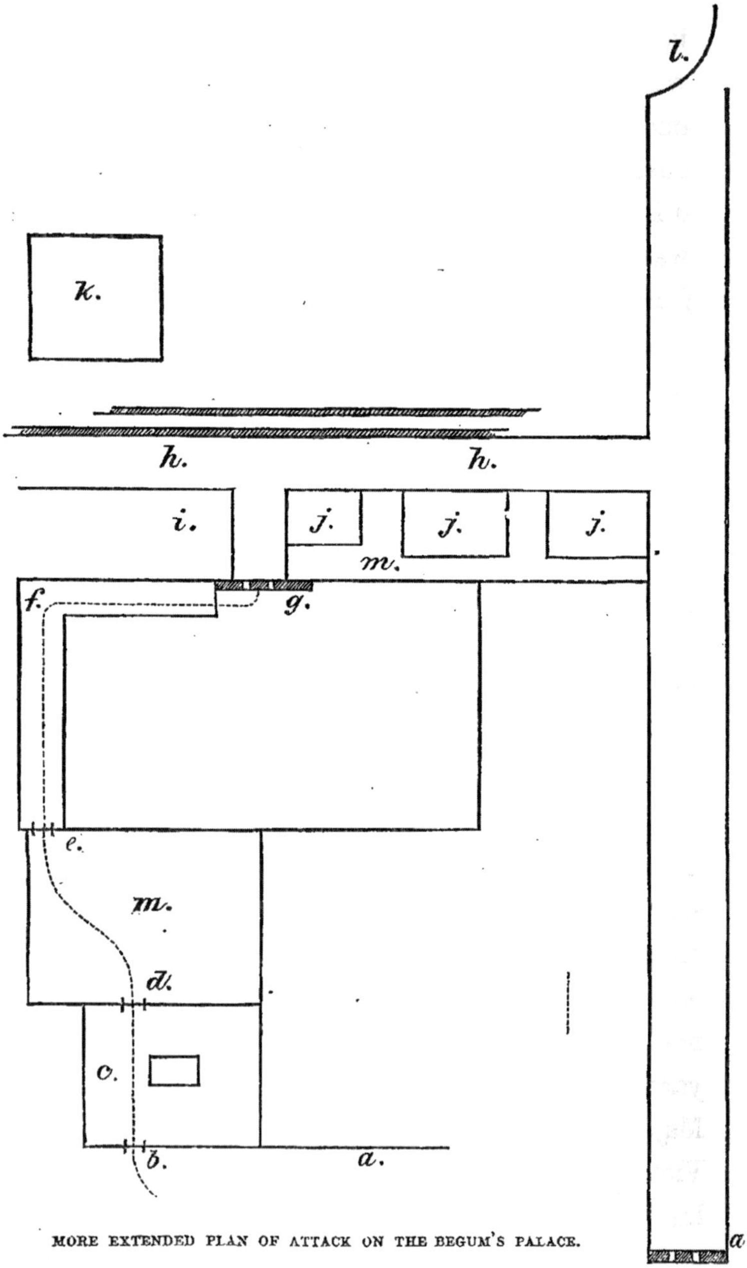

MORE EXTENDED PLAN OF ATTACK ON THE BEGUM'S PALACE.

is a large square building, containing but one room, which is used as a sort of mosque, and is profusely decorated with gilding and enormous coloured glass chandéliers: *l* is a Sepoy semi-circular battery, and *o* is the battery we took possession of yesterday. I was not on duty, so I went with Kerr into the house *j*, nearest to *k*, to reconnoitre; suddenly we heard a yell and a cheer, and the Sepoy bugles from two different quarters sound successively the alarm, the assembly, the advance, and the double; Kerr and I rushed back to our guns at *g*, the skirmishers evacuated their advanced post, and also fell back upon the guns, where we found all the troops drawn up under arms, the officers with swords drawn and pistols in hand; we waited for a few minutes in breathless anxiety, but the Sepoys only set on fire the house *i*, and then retired. I waited until our guns again opened fire, and was then compelled to return into camp; immediately after my departure, some sand-bags, forming the front of our battery, caught fire. A coloured man, of the name of Hall, a Canadian, gallantly jumped out and extinguished some, and threw far away others that were burning; in the performance of this exploit, under a heavy fire of bullets from loopholes not forty yards distant, he was severely wounded, and Her Majesty has since been pleased to award to him the Victoria Cross; he was always a man remarkable for his steady, good conduct, and his athletic frame; at a foot-race in camp, he had distanced by far all competitors, and I have never seen his superior either as a swimmer or diver. This evening we buried poor Garvey under some cypress trees in the garden of the Dilkushah; all the brigade in camp attended the funeral, and many military officers to whom he had endeared himself by his frank and affectionate character.

☉ *March* 14*th.*—This morning, having advanced our guns to within fifty yards of the Imaum-barah, it was captured with very little loss. At about noon I rode down towards our guns with Captain Vaughan, Kerr, and Lascelles, when we saw two or three officers on horseback, apparently unable to find their way across the canal; Kerr suddenly called out, "Why that is Sir James Outram," and so indeed it proved to be; he had crossed the lower bridge over the Goomtee, ridden past the Residency and through the Kaiser Bagh into our lines; we directed him to the head-quarters, and rode on. The rebels had only prepared for the attack on the town from the direction of the Dilkushah, and had thrown up three strong lines of defence in that direction; but Sir James Outram, crossing the river, not only attacked the town on the side on which it was almost totally undefended, but enfiladed the defensive works, one after the other. On arriving at our guns we dismounted, and proceeded on foot, leaving our horses to the care of our syces; we passed through the court of the Imaum-barah, which was strewn with the dead and dying, through breaches in walls and fortifications, through the remains of Oriental gardens, and through all the horrible indications of the recent skirmishing, until, on nearing the Kaiser Bagh, we met Sir Colin Campbell; he desired Captain Vaughan to bring up a gun's crew of blue-jackets to man an abandoned gun, which was to be turned against the retreating enemy; Kerr was sent back for the gun's crew, and we proceeded on to the gun itself, which was at a gate of an outer court of the Kaiser Bagh. We found that a body of Sepoys were defending themselves in an adjoining court, and it was necessary to blow away the gate of it that the troops might storm, and it was for this object that Sir Colin ordered the guns to be turned against them; in the meanwhile, however, they kept up a continual fire on us from the walls over and round the gate when we approached the gun. Captain Vaughan then fired a few rounds at the gate, I sponging and loading, three of the Shannon's bandsmen bringing up the powder and shot, and some men of the 38th, under command of Lieut. Elles, running the gun up after every round; our position at this time was very hazardous, as on our right was a house containing very large quantities of gunpowder, in some rooms lying in loose heaps on the floor three or four feet high, and in others contained in huge earthen chatties; moreover, the adjoining house to this was in flames, probably purposely kindled by the Sepoys; a sentry was, however, posted to give warning in time, if the flames approached the loose powder. Captain Vaughan now went back to meet the gun's crew that had been sent for, and to show them the way, leaving orders with me to keep up the fire; the Sepoy charges were so heavy that the shot went clean through the solid gate every time we fired, merely leaving a small loophole, through which the enemy fired at us; by reducing the charges with every shot, the firing at last began to tell; when the party of blue jackets came up, under command of Lieut. Hay, the gate was blown open, and the court captured by the company of the 38th. I then proceeded further to explore the palace: I forced open the large door of a building, which I discovered to be the King of Oude's coach-house; this was full of carriages, some of which were very curious; one was a long car, a sort of roofless omnibus, with gaudy decorations, very like the car drawn by an elephant, a cameleopard, and a pair of ostriches, which heads the procession of a travelling menagerie making its triumphal entry into a quiet country town. But there was one carriage, evidently the work of European hands, of a style of magnificence that I have never beheld before or since: all parts of the carriage, the wheels, the springs, and the frame, that are usually painted and varnished, were covered with thick plates of solid silver, and the appearance of the whole was perfectly dazzling, as the brilliant sunlight of an Indian spring poured upon it; the inside and the cushions were covered with the richest white silk, and in the box stuck a silver whip, with a lash of silver wire, of which I possessed myself. About an hour afterwards, I again passed this coach-house; the white silk had all been cut or torn off and carried away, nearly all the silver had disappeared, with the exception of one or two places where men were busily engaged hammering it off. I now climbed on to the roof of a neighbouring house to try and gain some idea of the geography of the palace: at my feet was a garden, on the opposite side of which stood another house; four or five men were running among the bushes, exchanging shots with men in the opposite house; at first it was difficult to tell which were English and which Sepoys, but the men in the garden soon came directly under me; they did not perceive me looking down on them, but I saw that *they* were Sepoys, and could easily have shot one had I had my revolver, but I carried only my sword; at last two of them were shot, and the remainder escaped through a side door.

After this I went over some portions of the Kaiser Bagh, but really an attempt to describe it would be vain: my wildest dreams of Oriental splendour were more than realised: I saw luxury, wealth, priceless silks, cashmeres, pictures, gilding, glass, and china, to an extent I hardly believed to have existed, and room after room was fitted up in a style of lavish magnificence devoid of taste: the principal court of the palace was of very great extent, containing gardens, aviaries, and conservatories; in the centre was an artificial lake spanned by a bridge of white marble, and lined all round with the same; at one end stood a pavilion of the most beautiful coloured marbles, and at the other a white marble mosque, much discoloured, however, by fire. I entered a detached building in flames, which had been used as an armoury, and in spite of the great heat, succeeded in bringing out a helmet of Damascus steel inlaid with gold, and having Persian characters worked on various parts of it; hence also I brought away a tulwa, some bows and arrows, a powder-horn of inlaid mother-of-pearl, and two standards: I also found a long straight sword of very curious workmanship, and meeting my servant I gave it him to carry up to camp for me; a quarter of an hour later he was walking with another man, when three Sepoys attacked him; they had no arms but this sword, and with it they killed one Sepoy and put the the others to flight; my sword, however, was broken, and my servant severely wounded in the hand. Shortly afterwards I met a doolie-wallah carrying a red standard with the King of Oude's arms embroidered on it in gold: now I thought that this being a trophy of war, was hardly a proper possession for a non-combattant, and I suggested this to him; as he made no opposition he apparently viewed the matter in the same light, so, with as little discourtesy as possible, I seized it. In another part of the garden, I saw a crown lying on the ground; it was made of cardboard and red satin, stiffened with rusty iron wire, and sewn all over with dull white beads; it appeared to have been used either for private theatricals or for a child's toy: I tore off half a dozen of the beads which I put into my pocket as mementos of the day. I saw a room full of little cabinets, every cabinet was full of little drawers, and every drawer was full of little bottles containing scents and spices, some were liquid and some solid; some agreeable and some very nasty, some like pills and others like their concomitants, but as there were none that I liked, I left them for the next comer. I met a

FAC-SIMILE OF GOLD COIN.

man with a little bag full of gold coins, which he had just found and bought one for half a sovereign; at last, thoroughly wearied out, I returned to camp, and gave away the beads I had plucked off the tawdry crown; but imagine my astonishment, when I was told that they were most beautiful pearls. I afterwards received one of them back, and estimated, at a rough guess, that the whole crown must have been worth two thousand pounds.

CHAP. IX.

SIEGE OF LUCKNOW. — THE KAISER-BAGH. — THE RESIDENCY. THE GREAT IMAUM-BARAH. — STORY OF MRS. ORR.

☽ *March* 15*th.* — Two guns were advanced up to the mess-house, which was stormed and taken by the 42nd Highlanders. We hear that many lives have been lost by powder blowing up, which was left about loose in large quantities by the Sepoys, probably on purpose. One of our engineers, Henri, purchased a sword and belt from a Sikh for 1*l.*; the knowing Sikh had touched the hilt with a file to see if it was silver gilt, but finding it the same colour throughout, sold it: Henri was much astonished to find that the hilt and mountings of the scabbard and belt were all of solid gold; some jewels which had been inlaid in the hilt were extracted before he bought it.

♂ *March* 16*th.* — 3. P.M. Four guns were advanced and got into position in the Residency, and the Great Imaum-barah was captured. 7. Opened fire on the city with shells and rockets. This afternoon I went to the Kaiser Bagh with Lieut. Young, and we climbed to the top of a large building containing a throne room and hall of audience. Here was a gallery which had been used as a look-out place; but before we had been there many minutes, we found ourselves the centre of general attention; a number of Sepoys who were still hanging about the palace opened fire upon us: of course at that great elevation, and from their rude matchlocks, the shot were very erratic, but still on the whole we deemed it prudent to descend: in some storehouses at the base of the building we found large crates of crockery emblazoned with the King of Oude's arms, which had never been opened, and were evidently of French manufacture: we sent into camp as much as we needed for our own use; a day or two later I passed the same spot, and saw that the whole of this beautiful china had been wantonly smashed. From one of the rooms, I cut a couple of pictures out of their frames, but almost all of them had been destroyed or defaced by swords and bayonets. In one of the courts I picked up a plated bit mounted with the royal arms of Oude.

☿ *March* 17*th.*—Yesterday evening six of our guns were advanced to the Residency, where they now are, occasionally firing a shot over the town: all seems quiet, and there is a report that the inhabitants are going to ransom their city, and turn the Sepoys out. I have purchased several arms that have been looted in the city; amongst others an old flint lock fowling-piece the stock and barrel of which are most beautifully inlaid with silver and gold, the sights and flash-pan being of pure gold. I have been into the Dilkushah to see Captain Peel and to give him a tulwa which he asked me to procure for him; the halls of that palace were crowded with sick soldiers, most of whom were burnt all over from head to foot by the dreadful explosions that have taken place in the city; they were covered with cotton wadding, and by the side of each sat a native with a paper fan to keep off the flies: the sighs and groans of these poor fellows, reduced to mere pieces of burnt flesh, were those of men who literally felt life to be a burden, men without hope of recovery to whom death could be but a relief: the scene was most harrowing. Yesterday morning I went down from our battery in the Residency to the Goomtee with Lieut. Wilson, to have a bathe, but the river was so choked with Sepoy corpses that we could not make up our minds to jump in. Some of our men caught a goat, milked her and drank all the milk; I then asked for some, but they had none left; however they took her down to the Goomtee, where she drank her fill; they then passed a bowline round her horns, ran her up and down the battery half a dozen times, milked her again, and brought me the milk, which I drank; it was rather watery, but passable under the circumstances. In battery in the Residency we have suffered from a plague of flies; I never before appreciated how terrible a thing a plague of flies could be; they have been bred by the innumerable dead bodies of men and animals; the moment one sits down they settle on every exposed part of the body; they drown themselves in tea and gravy, immolate themselves on the end of cigars, accompany to one's mouth all one's food, and render sleep next to impossible: indeed the only way to obtain any rest is to get under a mosquito curtain; at about sunset the mosquitoes relieve guard, and the flies have their watch below. I was sent down to the Great Imaum-barah this afternoon to bring up a prisoner from the guard-room. Instead of going through the main street, I tried a short cut through the native town; I had not ridden five hundred yards from the Residency before I found myself an object of great attraction to numbers of budmashes who were skulking about the deserted town, and amused themselves by firing at me from every available window or door. This was not pleasant; so with my revolver in my hand I put my horse into a gallop and dashed along considerably at random, as in those narrow and tortuous streets it was not easy to keep one's dead reckoning; no one attempted to stop me, and I was considerably relieved when I saw the tall minarets of the Great Imaum-barah towering over my head, and heard the sentry's challenge. From these minarets a beautiful view of the city can be obtained, and its appearance is very picturesque from every house being built round a court containing trees, gardens, and sometimes fountains and greenhouses; thus, when viewed from any height, it looks like succession of gardens. The body of

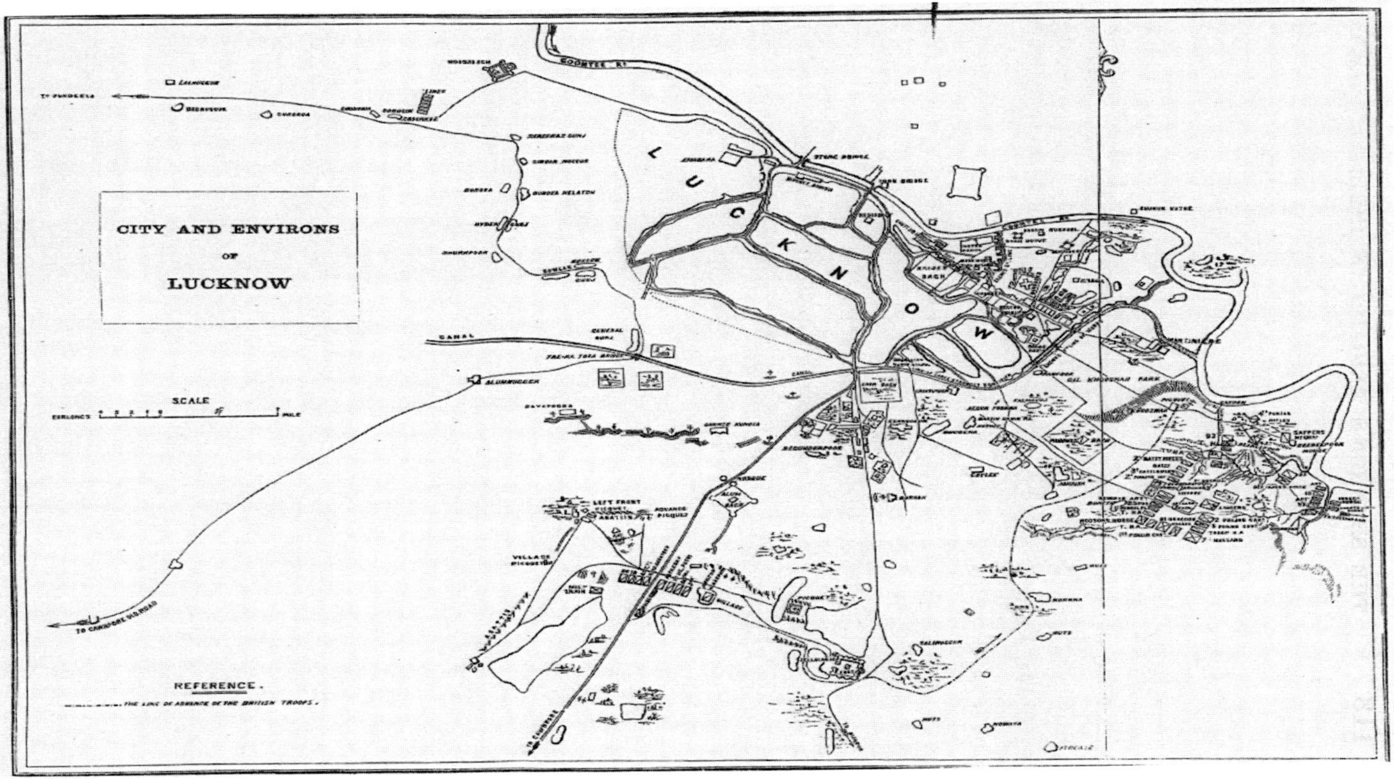
CITY AND ENVIRONS
OF
LUCKNOW
SCALE
MILE
REFERENCE.
THE LINE OF ADVANCE OF THE BRITISH TROOPS.
GOOMTEE R.
STONE BRIDGE
IRON BRIDGE
L U C K N O W
CANAL
ALUMBUGGER
LEFT FRONT PICQUET
ADVANCE PICQUET
VILLAGE PICQUETS
VILLAGE
GAL KHOORSHAD PARK
TO CAWNPORE

the building of the Great Imaum-barah, which is now used as a barrack, is of white stone, and remarkable for the extreme beauty of its architecture and the delicate tracery of its adornments; it contains a high pulpit covered with exquisitely embossed plates of silver, which is fortunately under the charge of a sentry.

☉ *March* 21*st.*—We have now in the Residency, four guns and eighty men, who are relieved every forty-eight hours: the town is all apparently quiet, but we know there are still many rebels about. Since we left Calcutta, a drill-sergeant of the 78th Highlanders has been attached to us; yesterday he was sent to rejoin his regiment, with a camel to carry his traps &c.: passing through a portion of the native town, at some distance from our guards, about a dozen Sepoys suddenly rushed out, killed the camel and its driver, and took his things: providentially he was following a little distance astern, and just escaped with his life.

☽ *March* 22*nd.*—The last body of rebels evacuated the town. I have visited the Shah Nujeef, and seen the spot where poor Daniel fell and was buried. The Sikhs are very knowing fellows: a Sikh serjeant will will watch a party of Europeans enter a house for the purpose of plundering, and immediately plant sentries all round, and as each man comes out, he is told that there are strict orders against looting, and that he must disgorge his plunder; this of course he does with a very bad grace, and walks away looking sadly crestfallen: as soon as the whole party have thus gone off, the sergeant calls in his sentries, divides the loot, keeping the lion's share for himself, and they all go on their way rejoicing.

March 25.—Captain Peel's wound is still going on favourably. To-day I visited the observatory, which was formerly one of the best in India: it is now little better than an empty house, a few rooms of which have been furnished for the use of General Sir Edward Lugard. When returning to camp, I passed two ladies in a carriage drawn by a pair of oxen; these were Mrs. Orr and Miss Jackson. Mrs. Orr saw her husband, Captain Orr, and Miss Jackson her brother, Sir Mountstuart Jackson, murdered by the Sepoys at the outbreak of the mutiny. These two ladies were then carried into Lucknow, where they have been kept until a few days ago when they were discovered and released by some English soldiers. The cruelties to which they have been subjected, are enough to extinguish any feeling of pity that one may retain for the rebels: at one time they were confined in a mud hut containing two rooms, in one of which they were placed while their guards occupied the other; they overheard the wretches talking and agreeing that it was quite right they should be killed, but neither was willing to do the deed: at last one of them got up and went away saying that he would leave the other to do it, and while they sat momentarily expecting their death, the other man arose and also departed, and thus at this time their lives were spared. When they were first made prisoners Mrs. Orr had a little daughter with her, in connection with whom occurred a remarkable manifestation of Divine Providence. Mrs. Orr first gave out that her child was sick and afterwards that it was dead, and it was then conveyed in a bundle of dirty linen to her brother-in-law in the Alumbagh by a faithful native; when she stated that it was sick, some medicine was given her for it, wrapped up in a piece of torn paper: on examining this, it proved to be a piece of the leaf of a large Bible, and on one side was written, "I, even I, am he that comforteth you; who art thou that thou shouldest be afraid of a man that shall die, and of the son of man which shall be made as grass: and forgettest the Lord thy maker, that hath stretched forth the heavens, and laid the foundations of the earth; and hast feared continually every day because of the fury of the oppressor, as if he were ready to destroy? and where is the fury of the oppressor?" and on the other side was written, "Thus saith thy Lord, the Lord, and thy God that pleadeth the cause of his people, Behold, I have taken out of thine hand the cup of trembling, even the dregs of the cup of my fury; thou shalt no more drink it again: but I will put it into the hand of them that afflict thee; which have said to thy soul, Bow down, that we may go over; and thou hast laid thy body as the ground, and as the street to them that went over."

Surely it is not presumption to regard this as a direct message of consolation from our Heavenly Father to one of His afflicted children.

♀ *March* 26*th.*—I rode down to the Residency to-day. A palace stands on the banks of the Goomtee called the Chutta Munzil, consisting of the usual conglomeration of courts, gardens, and rooms full of chandeliers; and through this a straight road has been cut to the Bailey Guard Gate of the Residency. I rode first through a court, then a hall, a throne-room, a garden, an artificial pond partially filled up, through more rooms, and at last out through a court and gateway, and it was by this road that our guns were brought up, and all subsequent supplies of ammunition, &c. When I returned, I rode along the banks of the Goomtee; the river was full of dead bodies that had caught among the weeds, and swamped near the Chutta Munzil was a miniature frigate, the ruined houses and palaces gave the city altogether a melancholy air of desolation.

♄ *March* 27*th.*—There is a wonderful rhinoceros in the camp, the property of the 53rd; he was found in Lucknow and is very tame; every day he is driven to a well to drink, guided by little taps from a twig which one would have thought could hardly have been felt through his thick hide: if, however, any one ventures to do more than touch him very lightly with it, he at once gets angry. He is very old, poor fellow, and suffers from some sort of ophthalmia, which has rendered him all but blind.

☉ *March 28th.* — Last night our four guns were withdrawn into park from the Residency. This morning Captain Peel has been out for a little exercise in a doolie, and is considerably better. One of our men, who was wounded in the thigh by a musket-ball, died last night of disease of the heart. Poor fellow! he was just recovering from his wound.

☾ *March 29th.*—Amongst other *souvenirs* of Lucknow, I have got from the palace a very handsome glass chandelier, with four branches; for each branch are two shades, one red and the other clear. We always use two branches; and when we have company to dinner four, which make our tent look very handsome. We hear that Captain Peel is going on as well as can be expected, but his severe wound will take some time to heal. To-day we have sent our two 8-in. howitzers and six 8-in. guns into park in the small Imaumbarah; the latter are the guns we brought from the Shannon, and we have now handed them over to the Artillery; and here they will remain, may I say it with pardonable pride, a memorial of what sailors *can* do on land. The word "Shannon" is cut deeply into each carriage, and must last as long as the wood does.

♂ *March 30th.*—A few days ago I was sent in to the Kaiser Bagh with ten men to bring out one of the King of Oude's carriages for Captain Peel's conveyance to Cawnpore. I selected the best I could find; and, having brought it into camp, our carpenters padded it, lined it with blue cotton, made a rest for his feet, and painted "H. M. S. Shannon" over the royal arms of Lucknow: when, however, he saw it to-day, he declined making use of it, saying that he would prefer to travel in a doolie like one of his blue jackets.

CHAP. X.

RETURN OF THE NAVAL BRIGADE.—BULLOCK-TRAIN TRAVELLING IN BENGAL.—DEATH OF SIR WILLIAM PEEL.—PUBLIC RECEPTION OF THE NAVAL BRIGADE AT CALCUTTA.

♃ *April 1st.*—This morning at 2 A.M. we struck tents, and passing in the dark through the sleeping camp commenced our march to Cawnpore. Yesterday, in the Kaiser-Bagh, I got a two-wheeled vehicle called a buggy out of the King of Oude's stables, emblazoned with his arms. I have harnessed one of my ponies to it, and it does capitally for carrying crockery and light baggage.

♀ *April 2nd.*—At 2 A.M. struck tents and proceeded on the march, encamping again at 6·30 on the Lucknow side of Bunny Bridge, which spans the only river between Lucknow and the Ganges. We have this morning had our first taste of the hot winds, and most remarkably like the continued blast of a furnace do they feel.

☉ *April 4th.*—Encamped at Unao.

☾ *April 5th.*—This morning Captain Vaughan went away with two companies and two guns to see after some rebels in a neighbouring village. In the meantime we are encamped under the trees of a snug little garden, whose walls afford some protection from the dust and hot winds. At night we have to send out picquets, which is rather dull work.

♂ *April 6th.*—This morning we marched into Cawnpore. A general order of this evening directs that arrangements be made for sending the Naval Brigade down to Calcutta by bullock-train, which will probably be a journey of about three weeks. Our two guns which left Unao yesterday morning found that the rebels had fled, so they had merely a man-of-war's cruise "there and back again;" the Sepoys were, however, chased by some Sikh cavalry, who cut them up a good deal. We are to leave here all the remainder of our battery. I have seen the monument erected over the well into which the bodies of the murdered women and children were thrown. This plain and beautiful memorial consists of a stone cross bearing the inscription: "In memory of the women and children of the 32nd Regiment, who were slaughtered near this spot 16th July, A.D. 1857. This memorial was raised by thirty men of the same regiment who were passing through Cawnpore, Nov. 21st, 1857." Round the circle by which the cross is connected is written: "I believe in the resurrection of the body."

☿ *April 7th.*—To-morrow at 3 A.M. we leave Cawnpore for Calcutta; we depart in three detachments: the first company and the Marines go to-morrow, under command of Lieut. Young; the officers are Captain Gray and Lieut. Stirling, R.M., Lieuts. Wilson and Wratislaw; Way and Richards, midshipmen, and myself. I am sorry to say that one of our midshipmen, Lord Arthur Clinton, is lying dangerously ill at the house of the Rev. T. Moore, the excellent chaplain of this station; another midshipman, Way, is, and has been for a long time very unwell. Among the arms I have brought from Lucknow is a tulwa of Damascus steel inlaid with a verse of the Koran in gold; a native gentleman here assures me that it must have cost at least 2000 rupees (200*l.*); I have also a cashmere dressing-gown, which must have been once worth a hundred pounds, although it is now old, worn out, and moth-eaten.

♃ *April 8th.*—This afternoon we have halted for dinner about twelve miles from Cawnpore, which, we left at 3 A.M.; we have drawn up the officers bullock waggons a little on one side of the road, among some trees; we have spread out our dinner-table on the altar of a picturesque little road-side temple, while a stream running close by furnishes us with water for cooking or bathing, and is most grateful to the eye and ear; we tarry here until the great heat of the day is passed.

♄ *April 10th.*—Allahabad. We arrived here yesterday evening at about nine, and took up our quarters at the permanent camp; our tents are wonderfully different to what we have been accustomed to up country, far more luxurious: the one in which I am is divided by a curtain into a dressing and sleeping room, and is double all round; the air between the inner and outer tent, being most efficacious in keeping us cool. Yesterday we had a specimen of how things are managed in India; we reached Futtehpore at about 10 A.M., and immediately an officer was sent to the railway station to report our arrival, with the number of men and amount of baggage requiring conveyance; in the meantime a letter came, ordering us to be there by three, to go down to Allahabad in the same train with Sir Colin Campbell; accordingly at about half-past two we arrived at the terminus, and found a small train near the platform capable of containing one hundred and twelve men; there was also a long train of trucks containing guns and ammunition waggons which a very stupid baboo was landing with a few coolies, and a great deal of noise, at the rate of one in twenty minutes: our commanding officer went from one railway official to another, but nobody seemed to know anything about us, or care whether we reached Allahabad or not; he went to the military and commissariat authorities, but they seemed afflicted with the same inertia as everyone else, and said that if there was not room for us all in this train, they supposed we must leave an officer behind to bring the rest of the men on in some other; so when Lieut. Young saw we could get no satisfaction out of any of them he set all our blue jackets to work, and in less than half an hour they had cleared every gun and ammunition waggon from the long train, and stowed all our own baggage in the trucks, and thus we all got down to Allahabad together. Sir Colin Campbell came down in the same train with us, and made a very complimentary speech to our men, who cheered him heartily. To-day the second detachment of the Naval Brigade arrived under command of Capt. Vaughan. Lord Canning, the Governor-General, is here.

☉ *April* 11*th.*—5·30 P.M. The third detachment arrived under command of Lieut. Hay. 6. The first detachment started by bullock-train for Benares.

♂ *April* 13*th.*—8 A.M. Halted for breakfast under a tope of trees. 1 P.M. Proceeded. 7·30. Arrived at Benares, and took up our quarters at the Mint.

♃ *April* 15*th.*—6 A.M. The second detachment, under Captain Vaughan, arrived by bullock-train. I have seen a field devoted to what in England would be considered a very extraordinary purpose, namely, the manufacture of ice. The whole field was full of square holes about six inches deep, and between every two was an earthen jar; in the winter, commencing in November, these holes are filled with straw, covered with about fifty shallow earthen-ware saucers; the jars are then filled with water, from which the saucers are filled with a large ladle; the water in the saucers will not freeze unless the straw is kept perfectly dry; early in the morning, the ice is taken out, pounded into lumps, and then put into the ice-houses; if a small piece of pottery accidentally gets in with it, it will eat its way to the bottom of the pit. It freezes at Benares about ten nights in the year, during which time, sufficient ice is made to last the inhabitants all the hot season.

♀ *April* 16*th.*—The building in which we are quartered was formerly the Mint, and still retains its name though now converted into barracks. We are waiting here for conveyance, all the bullock-waggons being detained somewhere between this and Raneegunge. The day before yesterday, we had a specimen of a real dust-storm; in the evening we first saw a thick brown cloud advancing from the north. Immediately every window was closed and door shut, and presently the air was so darkened that it was impossible to see the road; clouds of dust were whirled round and round, and the ground was soon covered with leaves torn from the trees. At length the storm seemed to abate a little, when suddenly a rushing sound was heard, and the ground became perfectly white with hailstones, many of them as large as a good-sized marble; after a time it all subsided, leaving the air clear, calm, and deliciously cool.

♄ *April 17th.*—9 A.M. The detachment under Lieut. Hay arrived.

☉ *April 18th.*—4 P.M. Proceeded by bullock-train across the bridge of boats over the Ganges towards Calcutta.

♂ *April 20th.*—8 A.M. Arrived at Sasseram, a large but squalid village containing one or two interesting ruins of mosques. 4 P.M. Half the detachment, under command of Lieut. Young, proceeded by bullock-train.

♃ *April 22nd.*—This morning at 6 A.M. we arrived at Shergotty: a telegraph has arrived directing us all to rendezvous at Raneegunge, as the council at Calcutta desire to give us a public reception. It is very gratifying that the services of the Naval Brigade, especially at the relief of Lucknow, are to be publicly recognised. Marching by bullock-train is not bad fun when one gets used to it, although bullock-waggons are not provided with springs. Carriage is provided for only two-thirds of the men, but for all the officers; one waggon drawn by two bullocks is allowed for every fifteen men; into this their bags and traps are put and ten men get in; the remaining five march as a van and rear-guard and are relieved every four hours; the bullocks are changed about every ten miles. There is one waggon for every two officers, and all are supplied with roofs and curtains at the sides. The perils and dangers of bullock-train travelling are as follows: between two stages a bullock may take it into his head to lie down, and thus he will insist on remaining, regardless of pricks, blows, or blandishments until such time as he sees fit to get up; the consequence is that the unfortunate inhabitants of the waggon are deprived of their rest, and do not reach the next station until it is time to leave it again. Or a bullock may be frightened or pretend to be frightened at anything or nothing, and will rush violently off the road, in spite of all the "bile-wallah" can do to stop him, down an embankment, into a river or swamp, sometimes overturning the waggon; such an animal becomes known as a "bobbery-bile," one of our men lost his life in consequence of an accident of this kind: on these occasions the whole train has to be stopped, the guards assemble and drag the waggon or what is left of it on to the road again. Or a wheel or pole may break, and then the contents of that waggon have to be transferred to some other, until some place is reached where one may be procured. Or a bile-wallah may fall asleep, and this may lead to any of the afore-mentioned calamities. A bullock-train generally starts at about 4 P.M. and averages two miles an hour. Half an hour before sunset, a couple of servants descend from the waggons, and run on ahead with a bundle of wood and a large kettle; they select a snug spot by the road side near a stream, light the fire, fill the kettle, and put it on; when the last waggon of the train reaches them, the "halt" is sounded, and grog served out to the men; the moment the water boils, perhaps in ten minutes or a quarter of an hour, the "advance" is sounded, the waggons move on, and the officers remain behind to drink their tea; then the servants gather up the traps, and run after and catch up the train. The van and rear guards are now told off for the night, and the men and officers walk by their waggons smoking and yarning, or at once turn in. The first attempt to sleep in a bullock-waggon is rarely successful, for once or twice during the night the bullocks are changed, and it requires practice to sleep through the shouts of the "bile-wallahs," the glaring of the torches, the bellowing of oxen, or occasional anathema of a blue jacket whose temper is put to a more than usually severe test. But all welcome the first rays of dawn, the singing of birds, and the delicious feeling of the fresh morning air, to which many a man passes his whole life a stranger; there is no more exhilarating hour of the four-and-twenty than this, when all nature around seems bounding with life and enjoyment of the mere act of living, and at no time is the heart more filled with gratitude to the great Creator for the bountiful provision He has made, not only for man's necessities, but for his enjoyment, in clothing this earth with such all-pervading beauty. Now beds are rolled up and stowed, and we stop behind at any brook we pass to enjoy a hasty wash, catch the train up again, and so proceed joyfully on our way, until we reach a station about noon; here sheds, erected on purpose, receive the men, and the dâk-bungalow the officers, and after due attention to the toilette we assemble for the one meal of the day, and four hours welcome rest. This is bullock-train travelling in Bengal.

♀ *April 23rd.*—Chumparun. We arrived here this morning; the last part of our journey has been through very hilly country, and we had great difficulty in getting the heavy bullock-waggons up the hills, some parts of which, covered with thick jungle, were very picturesque; they form part of the Rajmahal range. The day before yesterday we saw a few hills, but were not in a hilly country; it appeared more like a plain with hills stuck on afterwards.

♂ *April 27th.*—Burkutta. We are now about sixty miles from Shergotty, on the road to Calcutta, from which last place we are distant two hundred and thirty-three miles. Yesterday we had a sudden whirlwind of rain, dust, and hail, which blew away my writing portfolio, and scattered its contents far and wide. We arrived here on Saturday, and on Sunday proceeded forty miles further to a place called Nimiah Ghaut, where we received an express, ordering us to return to this place. We hear that Koor Sing has crossed the Ganges with a force of four thousand five hundred men; five hundred men of the Indian Navy were sent against him, but were entirely cut to pieces and their guns captured. We have, therefore, been ordered to remain here until the whole of the 6th shall have passed up, and then we are to return to Shergotty. We are now in three detachments: this one is under the command of Lieut. Young; Captain Vaughan commands another at Gyah; and the third is at Shergotty, under the command of Lieut. Wilson. The aspect of the country has entirely changed since we left Shergotty, having become picturesque and hilly.

☿ *April 28th.*—To-day we have had another storm and whirlwind, but not such a bad one as the last. The first detachment of the 6th Regiment arrived by bullock-train from Calcutta this morning, and will proceed in the evening; we have no proper barracks here, but our men have to put up in open sheds, while we live in the public room of the dâk-bungalow; at about 10 A.M. every day, a detachment arrives by bullock-train on its way up country, with perhaps four or five officers; to these we, of course, show all the hospitality in our power, and they remain with us until about 4 P.M., when they take their departure, and we are alone until the following forenoon. We live in a delicious air among the hills, and, though far from cool, have not the oppressive heat that we have elsewhere experienced; if the sun was a little less hot and burning, we might enjoy expeditions and pic-nics among the hills. I heard a reason assigned for the mutiny the other day, which was new to me;

the King of Oude was in the habit of keeping all men in his employ — soldiers, officers, or civilians — two or three years in arrears of pay; but when Oude was annexed, the king declared that he had no money wherewith to pay these arrears, and the Company refused to do so, on the ground that they had not contracted the debt, and so it remained unpaid. Now all these creditors had brothers, cousins, or near relations in the Sepoy regiments, and some of the Sepoys themselves were amongst the creditors; this gave rise to a feeling of discontent, which, if it did not cause the mutiny, at least exercised no small influence over the excited minds of the mutineers; the rebels thought they had a better chance of revenge against the Company than against the ex-king of Oude snugly ensconced at Calcutta.

♃ *April* 29*th.*—To-day another detachment of the 6th has passed up, and we hope to get away on Sunday evening. Although we shall only go as far as Shergotty, we shall be sixty miles nearer to the actual seat of war. It is curious to see how independent the Naval Brigade is, compared with infantry regiments; the Naval Brigade can be sent anywhere with a small body of cavalry, but an infantry regiment must be accompanied by detachments of artillery, cavalry, and sappers and miners. Now, with all humility, I would venture to suggest that the following staff of ten men might with advantage be attached to every regiment of foot, as every man-of-war carries a certain complement of artificers; and as, when any heavy work is to be done on board of a particular ship, all the artificers of other ships in company are sent to her, so, when three regiments are brigaded together, they might have a superior staff of thirty skilled artificers for employment in building bridges, pontoons, temporary barracks, &c.: 1. There might be a serjeant, understanding something of the trades of each of the nine men under his orders, and receiving good pay. 2. There should be a wheelwright, who in a few hours might build up some sort of waggon for conveying *materiel*, and, besides having the general supervision of all vehicles attached to the regiment, would be always able to assist other carpenters. 3. A shipwright, who could construct punts for a bridge of boats, have some sort of idea of sailorising, and be able to assist other carpenters. 4. A cabinet-maker, understanding fine work, who might be of great use in keeping barrack furniture in repair, and store-chests in the field, but able to assist in heavier work if required. 5. A caulker and cooper, who would assist in making pontoon bridges. 6. A house-carpenter, who would help the cabinet-maker, and might add much to the comfort of men in barracks by making rough articles of furniture. 7. A mason, who could use a spade and assist in throwing up an earthwork. 8, 9. An armourer and blacksmith, men whose trades are perhaps more different than is generally supposed, and without whose assistance carpenters would make but slow progress; the former of these would, of course, have the care of all spare arms, &c. 10. A painter, whose trade is quite as useful as ornamental, as no permanent woodwork ought to be exposed to the weather without a coat of paint. Major Guise, of the 90th, bought a very good double-tent, but the piece of wood which kept the two roofs apart was accidentally broken; so the tent became very hot, indeed, quite unbearable, and no one was able to repair it until Captain Vaughan sent one of our carpenters, who fitted another piece of wood, and put it all to rights in an hour. A sovereign was considered a fit recompense for this hour's work.

♀ *April 30th.*—To-day we have been much distressed to learn the death of our noble captain. He fell a victim to small-pox on the 27th, when just recovering from his wound; he refused to go from Lucknow to Cawnpore in the carriage that was prepared for him, saying that he would sooner travel in a doolie like one of his blue jackets, and it is supposed that his doolie must have been previously used for a small-pox patient. The information was brought by Lieut.-Col. Wells, V.C., of the 23rd, as he passed us on his way down to Calcutta. I cannot say what a sad loss we all feel this to be, and how deeply his death is felt and regretted by every officer and man; the mainspring that worked the machinery is gone. We never felt ourselves to be the *Shannon's* Naval Brigade or even the *Admiralty* Naval Brigade, but always *Peel's* Naval Brigade. He it was who first originated the idea of sailors going one thousand four hundred miles away from the sea, and afterwards carried it out in such an able and judicious manner. I do not doubt that his worth will be appreciated and his death deeply lamented by the people of England.

Burkutta is the most retired, out-of-the-way place it is possible to imagine. It is true that troops arrive day after day; but, as they have been perhaps a week on the road, they look to us for news. Occasionally some one, travelling down rapidly by horse-dâk, flashes upon us like a meteor, perhaps leaving behind him some shadowy scattered piece of news, delivered with an air of the most vital importance, such as "*Koor Sing has crossed the river; good bye*," and instantly the carriage dashes on again. What river? when? who heard him say so? Nobody knows. It may be that he has crossed back again to the east side of the Ganges; or our informant may have only just become aware of his having crossed at all; or it may be that he has crossed the Soane, coming south, or going north; or it may be that the eyes of all India are fixed (metaphorically) on the banks of some river of which we have as yet heard nothing: so we shut out the big world altogether, as being, under the circumstances, beyond our comprehension; and we concentrate our hopes and fears on the few sheds containing the little garrison of Burkutta. This place is really so small, that the post-office authorities will not even recognise its existence; the one European resident has his letters directed to a friend at Shergotty, who kindly sends them back in a waggon. By the following method we keep our rooms tolerably cool:—The wind blows steadily all day with scorching heat from one point of the compass: the windward door is stopped up by a thick mat called a "tatty," made from the root of the "cuscus" grass, strengthened with bamboo. Outside sits a native with a large tub of water by his side, and from this he continually sprinkles the mat, keeping it always wet. The hot wind blowing through it is effectually cooled by the evaporation; and, by using a punkah at the same time, a room may be made almost cold.

From this date my continuous journals of the proceedings of the Shannon's Naval Brigade cease. On the 4th of May the detachment with which I was serving left Burkutta, arriving at Shergotty on the 6th. On that same evening I again left for Calcutta with a arge party of sick and invalids, and returned to the Shannon on the 12th of May.

June 13th.—Lieut. Young, writing from Shergotty, says: "They are at last building barracks for us here, but they cannot be finished for a month. The heat has been excessive, 102° at night in the coolest bungalow in the place. One of our poor fellows, Flynn, a foretopman, actually died of the heat; he went to bed all right and sober, and by all accounts had not been in the sun, but was found a few hours afterwards in a dying state, with the symptoms of sunstroke.

☿ *June* 30*th.*—This evening Captain Marten, who has been appointed acting captain of the Shannon, went up country to take command of the Naval Brigade, taking with him Mr. Digby, naval cadet, as his A.D.C.

♂ *July* 27*th.*—This morning I left the Shannon with Mr. L. P. Willan, naval cadet and thirty-five men, as a reinforcement to our Brigade at Gyah, and in the afternoon reached Raneegunge by rail.

☿ *July* 28*th.*—This afternoon left Raneegunge by bullock-train.

♃ *July* 29*th.*—5 A.M. Arrived at Toldangah. We are most thankful for fine weather, but the river Burâka, which I passed as an insignificant stream on my way, was this morning so swollen by the rains, that we had to cross it in ferry-boats. The stages have been shortened, so that now seven days are allowed for performing a distance, for which only five were previously granted; this makes our travelling more agreeable.

☉ *August* 1*st.*—At 5 A.M. we arrived at Burkutta,

and a note was put into my hand from Lieut. Young, ordering me to return to the ship, as the whole brigade is on its way down country, so this afternoon I start again for Calcutta.

☾ *August 2nd.*—Arrived at Doomree. A dog belonging to Captain Dansey, commissariat officer here, who showed us such cordial hospitality when we were at Burkutta in April, was killed last night by a leopard, it was therefore left in a field for bait, and when the animal came to devour it, he was shot by a native: he must have been a very fine fellow indeed, with enormous fangs and claws.

♃ *August 5th.*—Arrived on board the Shannon, in the middle of a shower of rain.

♃ *August 12th*—At 3 P.M. I crossed the Hooghly with all the Shannon's men, who served in the interior, to the railway station, to meet the Brigade coming down country: at five they arrived, we all formed together on the railway platform, and then embarked on board the steamer; a detachment under command of Lieut. Young was still in the interior, but altogether we numbered about two hundred and twenty: as we steamed across the Hooghly, all the ships in that mighty stream dressed with flags, some bearing the word "Welcome;" on reaching the opposite pier we were enthusiastically cheered, the wharves were decorated with flowers, flags, and evergreens, surmounted by the inscription "Welcome, hearts of oak," all the houses on the Strand, as far as the Shannon, a distance of about a mile were similarly decorated, the road was lined by almost the entire population of Calcutta, European and native: all the thoroughfares leading to the Strand were blocked up and a double row of native policemen, dressed in white with red turbans and cummerbunds, kept the road. We landed on the pier, and passing between two rows of ladies, formed on the road; the order "fours right," was then given, and we marched off, our band leading, escorted in front and rear by the Calcutta Volunteer Cavalry: Fort William saluted with twenty-one guns, and the people all cheered as we passed, the ladies showering down flowers and bouquets on us: at length we emerged on the Maidân, the public promenade, where the road on each side was lined with carriages, the horses unharnessed, and troops who presented arms as we passed; amongst others were the 77th, the Calcutta Volunteer Guards, the Calcutta Volunteer Artillery, the Calcutta Volunteer Rifles, the Indian Naval Brigade, the ship's company of H.M.S. Pylades, Captain M. de Courcy and small remnant of the crew of H.M.S. Pearl, who were still serving in the interior under Captain Sotheby. A bridge of boats had been constructed from the shore to the Shannon's gangway, and each company marched on board and fell in on the quarter-deck as if they had been on shore for a day's drill instead of a year's service. The order was given to "ground arms" and then the pipe rang through the decks, "hands cheer ship;" in a moment our lower and topmast rigging were swarming with men and three such mighty English cheers rolled over that old Maidân, as the Indian soil had never echoed to before, and probably never will again. And where all this time was our old companion in arms who had planned our enthusiastic reception, Sir James Outram, well named the Bayard of India? As we stepped over the gangway of the Shannon, perhaps we hardly noticed a figure dressed in the plainest of plain clothes, whose eagle eye scanned every bronzed face as it appeared, welcoming one with a nod, and another with a cordial shake of the hand; yet this was Sir James Outram, and in this simple way did he welcome us all.

♂ *August 24th.*—This evening Sir James and Lady Outram gave a grand ball to the officers of the Shannon, at which almost the whole of Calcutta society was present.

☿ *August 25th.*—Lieut. Young returned on board with the remaining detachment of the Shannon's Naval Brigade.

☿ *September 1st.*—This evening a banquet was given in the Town Hall, to the seamen of the Shannon's Naval Brigade; it was attended by a large number of people, and several very fair speeches were made by our chief petty officers referring to the transfer of the government of India to the Crown, which took place to-day.

September 15*th.*—H.M.S. Shannon sailed from Calcutta.

CHAP. XI.

THE RETURN OF H.M.S. SHANNON TO ENGLAND. — PROMOTIONS AND DECORATIONS BESTOWED UPON HER OFFICERS AND BLUE JACKETS.

EARLY in the morning of the 15th of January 1858, H.M.S. Shannon sailed from Calcutta, under the command of Captain Marten. She touched at Trincomalee, and reached the Cape of Good Hope on the 6th of November: on the 13th she left the Cape, and touching at St. Helena and Ascension, anchored at Spithead on the 29th of December. The behaviour of her ship's company on the passage home was what might have been expected as the result of the fellow-feeling and mutual esteem engendered by the vicissitudes of an arduous campaign: and indeed it was no easy matter for her varied crew, many of whom had been merchant seamen, to fall in at once to the routine of a man-of-war; the ship was inspected in Portsmouth harbour by Sir George Seymour, the Port Admiral, the Naval Brigade passed before him in review order, and he addressed them in a short but hearty speech. The officers of H.M.S. Excellent entertained the officers of the Naval Brigade at dinner, on the 15th of January

1859, at 3·30 P.M. the last man of the Shannon's crew was paid off.

The officers of H.M.S. Shannon received the following promotions:—Lieut. Vaughan was promoted to the rank of commander, and after serving for one year, to that of captain; Lieuts. Young, Wilson, Hay, Salmon, and Wratislaw were promoted to the rank of commander; Dr. Flanagan, assistant-surgeon, was promoted to the rank of surgeon; Mr. Verney, mate, was promoted to the rank of lieutenant; Mr. Comerford, assistant-paymaster, was promoted to the rank of paymaster; and each of the engineers and warrant-officers received a step. To the midshipmen and naval cadets were promised their promotions to the rank of lieutenants on their passing the requisite examinations, which has in each instance been performed.

The Victoria Cross was presented to Lieuts. Young and Salmon and three blue jackets "for valour" at the relief of Lucknow, mentioned in despatches by Sir William Peel. Commander Vaughan received the order of C.B., an honour never before accorded to any naval officer below the rank of captain.

The Indian medal, with the Lucknow clasp, was presented to each officer and man who formed part of the Naval Brigade. The following officers, who were present at the relief of Lucknow, on the 17th of November, received also the "Relief of Lucknow" clasp:—Lieuts. Vaughan, Young, and Salmon; Capt.

Gray, R.M.; Rev. E. L. Bowman; Dr. Flanagan; Mr. Comerford, assistant paymaster; Messrs. M. A. Daniel, E. St. J. Daniel; Lord Walter Kerr, Lord Arthur Clinton, and Mr. Church, midshipmen: Messrs. Bone and Henri, engineers, and Mr. Bryce, carpenter. Never was medal more highly prized, or clasp more nobly won.

APPENDIX.

"Camp, Futtehpore,
"3rd November, 1857.

"SIR,

"I have the honor to lay before His Excellency the Commander-in-Chief the details of the battle of Khujwa with the circumstances that preceded it.

"Detachments amounting to 700 men under the command of Lieut.-Col. Powell, of H.M. 53rd Regiment, in charge of siege-train guns and a large convoy were proceeding from Allahabad to Cawnpore, and had arrived on the 31st of October, after a march of twelve miles, at the camping-ground of Thurrea. The same afternoon intelligence was received from Futtehpore that the sepoy mutineers of the Dinapore Regiment with three guns had passed the Jumna with the intention of either attacking Futtehpore or crossing over into Oude. The camp was immediately struck, and we arrived at the camping-ground of Futtehpore at midnight.

"Colonel Powell then made arrangements for marching at daylight upon the enemy, who were reported to be about twenty-four miles distant at Khujwa beyond the village of Binkee. The column of attack consisted of 162 men of H.M. 53rd Regiment under *Major Clarke;* 68 of the Royal Engineers under *Captain Clarke;* 70 of a depôt detachment under Lieutenant Fanning of H.M. 64th Regiment, and 103 of the Naval Brigade under Captain Peel. It marched at daylight and was joined from the garrison of Futtehpore by a company of the 93rd Highlanders, 100 in number, under Captain Cornwall, and two 9-pr. guns under Lieutenant Anderson, Bengal Artillery. After marching for sixteen miles, the column halted for refreshment and then resumed the march at a rapid pace passing the village of Binkee at about 1·30 P.M., when the intelligence was confirmed that the enemy was at hand.

"The troops pressed on without interruption, the Highlanders advancing in skirmishing order supported by the Royal Engineers and followed by the 53rd in column, and then by the Naval Brigade; the depôt detachment was with the baggage. We advanced along the road which led straight for the village of Khujwa and saw that the enemy's right occupied a long line of high embankments on our left of the road, which embankment, screened by a grove, continued towards the village, and that their left was higher upon the other side with their guns posted in the centre on the road, two of them in advance and one on a bridge near the village.

"A round shot coming down the road opened the battle at about 2·20 P.M. and the column was ordered to edge to the right and advance on the guns through the corn-fields. The skirmishers of the 93rd and the Royal Engineers pushing on both sides of the road. The enemy's artillery was well served and did great execution, and the flank fire of musketry was very severe. The gallant Colonel Powell himself on the left of the road, pressed on the attack, and had just secured two guns of the enemy when he fell dead with a bullet through his forehead.

"In the meantime the Naval Brigade had advanced on the right of the 53rd, and carried the enemy's position in their front. It was then that the death of Colonel Powell was reported to me, and I was requested to assume the command. The great force of the enemy, the long line of their defences, and the exhaustion of both officers and men after such long marches rendered our position truly critical. The front of the battle had become changed to the line of the road, and the enemy with all their force behind their embankments threatened to intercept our rear. I left Lieutenant Hay, R.N., supported by two 9-pr. guns to hold the position which his party had gallantly carried, and which secured our flank, and collecting as many fresh troops as were available, assisted principally by Lieutenant Lennox, Royal Engineers (Captain Clarke being unfortunately severely wounded), and by Ensign Small of the 53rd we marched across the road, and passing round the uppe end of the embankment divided the enemy's force and drove them successively from all their positions. The enemy then retired in confusion, leaving us masters of their camp and with two of their guns and a tumbril in our possession.

"The late hour of the evening (it was half-past four when the enemy fired their last shot), and the excessive fatigue of the troops prevented any pursuit; we therefore spoiled their camp, and leaving it with cheers, formed on the road by the bridge near the village, and sent out parties to collect our dead and wounded.

"With the body of the colonel on the limber of the gun he had so gallantly captured, we then returned and encamped near the village of Binkee. Our loss in the action was very severe, amounting to ninety-five killed and wounded. Enclosed are the returns of the column of attack.

"The behaviour of the troops and of the Naval Brigade was admirable, and all vied with each other and showed equal courage in the field. The marching of the 53rd, and the accurate firing of the Highlanders, deserved especial commendation.

"I received the greatest assistance from Captain Cox, H.M.

75th Regiment, whom I wish to bring to the favourable notice of H.E. the Commander-in-Chief; and the arrangements of the field-hospital, under Dr. Grant H.M. 53rd; and those of the Quarter-Master's department under Captain Marshall, were everything I could wish. The total number of the enemy was reported to be about 4000 men, 2000 of whom were sepoys, who fought in their uniform. Their loss was estimated at above 300 killed.

"I have the honour to be, Sir,

"Your very obedient servant,

(Signed) "WILLIAM PEEL, Capt., R.N., Commanding.

"I have the pleasure to inform His Excellency that the remaining gun of the enemy with three tumbrils was brought in this evening by the police, having been abandoned by the rebels in their flight about eight miles beyond Khujwa; and that the sepoys have dispersed in all directions pursued by the villagers."

EXTRACT FROM THE LONDON GAZETTE, *May* 25, 1858.

No. 17.—*Nominal Roll of Officers of Her Majesty's ship Shannon's Brigade serving under Captain Peel, K.C.B., who are deemed worthy of promotion, or of honourable mention, for their services during the campaign, and in the capture of Lucknow, March* 1858.

LIEUTENANT THOMAS J. YOUNG, gunnery officer of Her Majesty's ship Shannon.—This officer has been distinguished in every engagement by his cool courage and admirable skill as a gunnery officer: has been specially employed on all critical occasions, and has been named for the Victoria Cross. —Recommended for promotion.

Lieutenant NOWELL SALMON.—An excellent officer; distinguished himself in the Shannon's Brigade at the relief of Lucknow, was severely wounded, and named for the Victoria Cross.—Recommended for promotion.

Mr. EDMUND H. VERNEY, senior acting mate, zealous and well-conducted.—Recommended for promotion.

Officers not eligible for promotion, but worthy of honourable mention:—

Lord WALTER T. KERR, midshipman.—Has had an independent command.—Is very highly recommended.

Lord A. P. CLINTON, and Mr. E. J. CHURCH, midshipmen. —Have behaved admirably, and are very promising officers.

WILLIAM PEEL, Captain, R.N.,
Commanding Shannon's Naval Brigade.

Lucknow, March 31, 1858.

THE END.